WRITING

O

READING

D

SPELLING

STUDENT BOOK **3**

Louise Skinner

Dianne Tucker - LaPlount

 CAMBRIDGE Adult Education
A Division of Simon & Schuster
Upper Saddle River, New Jersey 07458

Executive editor: *Mark Moscowitz*
Editorial/production supervision: *Peggy M. Gordon*
Cover design: *Marianne Frasco*
Production coordinator: *Ed O'Dougherty*

 © 1995 by CAMBRIDGE Adult Education
A Division of Simon & Schuster
Upper Saddle River, New Jersey 07458

Printed in the United States of America

10 9 8 7 6 5 4 3 2 1

ISBN 0-13-953290-0

Prentice-Hall International (UK) Limited, *London*
Prentice-Hall of Australia Pty. Limited, *Sydney*
Prentice-Hall Canada, Inc., *Toronto*
Prentice-Hall Hispanoamericana, S.A., *Mexico*
Prentice-Hall of India Private Limited, *New Delhi*
Prentice-Hall of Japan, Inc., *Tokyo*
Simon & Schuster Asia Pte. Ltd., *Singapore*
Editora Prentice-Hall do Brasil, Ltda., *Rio de Janeiro*

Review of WORDS 2

PART 1

Work with the teacher.

Fill in each blank with the correct number.

	How many syllables?	How many vowel letters?	How many vowel sounds?
1. credit	2	2	2
2. lunch	___	___	___
3. donate	___	___	___
4. public	___	___	___
5. slope	___	___	___

Divide each word into syllables.

1. rubbish	rub	bish
2. contest	_____	_____
3. traffic	_____	_____
4. umpire	_____	_____
5. mistake	_____	_____
6. include	_____	_____

1

Add **sh** or **ch** to complete the words.

1. fla_sh_   **3.** ____est   **5.** ____rimp

2. ben____   **4.** cra____   **6.** bran____

Divide the words below into syllables. Mark the vowels. Each word has a short vowel sound in the first syllable and a schwa sound in the second syllable. Remember that the schwa sound is a weak /u/.* In the dictionary, the schwa looks like this: ə

Example: husband   həs bənd

1. gallon _____ _____   **3.** bottom _____ _____

2. absent _____ _____   **4.** sandal _____ _____

One of these words has a schwa sound in the second syllable. Circle that word.

contest   lesson   invite   zigzag

Write the word *open* after each open syllable. Write *closed* after each closed syllable. Mark the vowels long (-) or short (˘).

1. prī _____open_____   **4.** gla _____

2. ăb _____closed_____   **5.** est _____

3. səd _____   **6.** ro _____

Divide each word into syllables. Mark the vowel in the first syllable long (-) or short (˘).

1. cabin __căb'__ ____ĭn____   **4.** finish _____ _____

2. music _____ _____   **5.** planet _____ _____

3. veto _____ _____   **6.** lady _____ _____

Tch or ch? Make each word complete by filling in the blank with **tch** or **ch.**

1. scra ____   **2.** pi ____   **3.** ran ____

*In some places, the schwa is pronounced as a weak /ĭ/.

These words end with a **consonant + le** syllable. Divide each word into syllables.

Insert these sentences into the grid below.

1. Twenty people were standing in line at 6 A.M.

2. A rattlesnake can strike quickly.

3. The huge crate hit the sidewalk with a thud.

4. Your blue jacket is hanging in the hall closet.

	SUBJECT	VERB	OBJECT			
Which? Whose? How Many?	*Who? or What?*	*Does? Did? Will Do?*	*What? or Whom?*	*Where?*	*When? How Often? How Long?*	*How? Why?*
1.						
2.						
3.						
4.						

Sight words do not follow the rules of spelling and must be memorized. One of the words below is a sight word. Circle it.

contract   branch   athlete   people

Divide these compound words into syllables. Mark the vowels long (-) or short (ˇ). (Mark only the vowels that you *hear*.)

1. spaceship _____ _____   **3.** bathtub   _____ _____

2. bedtime   _____ _____   **4.** homesick _____ _____

Write these words in alphabetical order.

pamphlet   _____

prank   _____

plastic   _____

planet   _____

Add **s** or **es** to each of these words to form plurals (more than one).

1. fox ____   **5.** graph ____

2. path ____   **6.** brick ____

3. dress ____   **7.** bench ____

4. buzz ____   **8.** dish ____

Write the *irregular plurals* of these words.

1. man ____

2. woman ____

3. child ____

Work with the teacher.

Join each root word and its affix.

1. charge + ing = <u>   *charging*   </u>

2. hope   + ed = <u>   </u>

3. scrub + ed = <u>   </u>

4. shake + y   = <u>   </u>

5. use   + ing = <u>   </u>

6. hunt + ed = <u>   </u>

7. fog   + y   = <u>   </u>

8. hop   + ing = <u>   </u>

Complete each word below by filling in the blank with **ge** or **dge**.

1. bri ____   2. ju ____   3. hin ____

PART 2

Listen, then circle the word that the teacher says.

1. bash   batch   badge

2. stuck   stock   stoke

3. unit   unite   untie

4. crutch   crunch   crush

5. slide   slid   sled

6. trill   thrill   frill

Lesson 1

The Vowel Combinations **ay** and **ai**

AY as in DAY

Work with the teacher.

When you hear the long **a** sound at the end of a word, usually it is spelled **ay**.

Pronounce these words with the class or teacher.

say	may	way	today	stay
pay	sway	maybe	tray	play
ray	freeway	stray	lay	gray
delay	bay	slay	pray	decay
day	clay	spray	display	

Choose a word from the above box that matches a definition below. Write the correct word on the line.

1. _____ to postpone; to put off until later

2. _____ to kill

3. _____ a cove; an inlet

4. _____ to move from side to side

5. _____ to rot; to waste away

6. _____ mist; fine drops of liquid, such as water

6

Read with the teacher.

THE DAYS OF THE WEEK

The days of the week were named hundreds of years ago. The first two days were named after the sun and the moon. The other five were named after gods and a goddess of that time.

Sunday—day of the sun

Monday—day of the moon

Tuesday—day of Tiu, god of war

Wednesday—day of Woden, chief of the gods

Thursday—day of Thor, god of thunder

Friday—day of Fria, goddess of love and the sky

Saturday—day of Saturn, god of agriculture

Writing the short way: The seven days of the week often are abbreviated.

Sunday	Sun.
Monday	Mon.
Tuesday	Tues.
Wednesday	Wed.
Thursday	Thurs.
Friday	Fri.
Saturday	Sat.

Copy the above abbreviations and memorize them.

1. _____ 3. _____ 5. _____ 7. _____

2. _____ 4. _____ 6. _____

Read with the teacher.

The word *holiday* was made from two words: *holy* and *day*. In Old English, it meant a special day to celebrate a religious event. Today we pronounce the letter **o** with a short sound, and the letter **y** has been changed to **i**.

Read these word groups with the class or teacher.

a holiday in Dayton

parked in the driveway

at the daylong sale

fell by the wayside

and payday is today

a paycheck by midday

maybe on Tuesday

sometimes on Wednesday

but no pay for the holiday

MAVERICK: Study this sight word with the teacher.

says

Write the *pronunciation* of each of these words. Use the dictionary. The first one has been done for you.

1. maybe _(mā′ bē)_ **2.** says _____ **3.** Wednesday _____

Work with the teacher.

The word *always* comes from the Old English language. It used to mean *all the way*. Today it means *all the time*. It is *one* word, spelled with one **l**, with an **s** at the end.

Complete these sentences with the word *always*. Notice that this word can be used in different places within a sentence.

1. I _____ pay my rent on time.

2. Will you love me _____?

3. The foreman is _____ on the job by 7 A.M.

4. Candles _____ are lit in the chapel.

Make words with the **ay** vowel combination by using consonants. Do not make plural words. Work with the teacher. Write eight words.

_____pray_____

_____

_____

_____

_____

_____

_____

_____

Work with the teacher.

Draw a line between word groups in Column A and in Column B to form complete sentences.

Column A	**Column B**
1. The boss says that	always falls on a Thursday.
2. Will the store	in the driveway?
3. Thanksgiving	closed on holidays?
4. Is the post office	Wednesday is payday.
5. We drove to Dayton	display the items on sale?
6. Does Ray always park	last Friday.

Read these sentences with the class or teacher.

1. Is the nozzle plugged up on that spray can?

2. Freeway traffic was backed up for a mile.

3. By midday, the children were tired and hungry.

4. Most bricks are made of clay, but some are made of glass.

5. Strong winds may delay the plane from Bombay.

The teacher will dictate ten words.

1. _____
2. _____
3. _____
4. _____
5. _____
6. _____
7. _____
8. _____
9. _____
10. _____

AI as in RAIN

Work with the teacher.

The **ai** combination is pronounced /ā/. This combination is used either at the beginning or in the middle of a word. Most words with the **ai** spelling came into the English language from the French.

Pronounce these words with the class or teacher.

rain	chain	sail	wait	aim
train	stain	mail	bait	claim
brain	pain	snail	aid	faith
sprain	paint	rail	raid	raise
main	faint	trail	braid	praise

HOMOPHONES

Many words in English *sound alike* but are spelled differently and have different meanings. These words are called *homophones*. Discuss the meanings of the following homophones with the teacher.

mail	maid	pain	waist
male	made	pane	waste
sail	pail	tail	plain
sale	pale	tale	plane

Read each sentence and find the homophone that matches the word given in the parentheses. Write the homophone on the line after the sentence. The first one has been done for you.

1. (maid) Lee made fish sandwiches for lunch. _____*made*_____

2. (tale) That jet has a blue emblem on its tail. _____

3. (plane) He always dresses in plain clothes. _____

4. (sail) Those used cars are for sale. _____

5. (pale) The toddler dumped mud in a plastic pail. _____

6. (waist) Don't waste your money at the arcade. _____

7. (pane) She felt a dull pain in her left arm. _____

8. (male) Does express mail arrive in one day? _____

Work with the teacher.

Match each word in Column A with its definition in Column B. Write the letter of your answer on the line.

Column A	**Column B**
_e_ **1.** tail	**a.** bucket
____ **2.** aid	**b.** icy rain
____ **3.** wail	**c.** help
____ **4.** pail	**d.** path
____ **5.** jail	**e.** the end of something; the back part
____ **6.** mail	**f.** ill
____ **7.** ail	**g.** not strong
____ **8.** trail	**h.** prison
____ **9.** hail	**i.** post; letters and parcels
____ **10.** frail	**j.** cry

IRREGULAR VERBS

Study the following words. Notice that the affix **ed** is not added to the end of the words *pay, lay,* and *say* in the past tense. These are *irregular verbs*.

Base Form

pay   lay   say

Past Tense

paid (not payed)   laid (not layed)   said (not sayed)

Fill in each blank with the past tense of the word in parentheses.

1. The guard _____, "Wait here at the main gate."
                 (say)

2. Dr. Clayton _____ her glasses on the desk.
               (lay)

3. Mr. Millay grumbled as he _____ his phone bill.
                    (pay)

4. Fifty-five people were _____ off at the plant today.
               (lay)

WHAT'S MISSING?

Work with the teacher.

Read the sentences below with the class or teacher. Look at the beginning and the end of each sentence. Also check the abbreviations. Something is wrong or missing. Make the corrections.

1. i need a Band-Aid for this cut on my thumb.

2. why do some crazy drivers tailgate on the freeway.

3. mr. Grayson got off the train at Tenth and Parkway

4. are you going to ask for a raise

5. the basketball games always start at 7:30 P.M.

MAVERICK: Study this sight word with the teacher.

straight

Work with the teacher.

FOLLOWING DIRECTIONS

A *row* is a line of things. A row of words on paper usually goes from left to right across the page. Below are three rows of words. Read the words.

1. maintain ✓   complain   complaint

2. raisin   contain   rainfall

3. remain   straight   cocktail

In row 1, put a check after the first word. (This has been done for you.)

In row 2, put a check before the third word.

In row 3, put a check after the second word.

Work with the teacher.

Read these sentences with the class or teacher.

1. Carlos drove straight home from the Mayo Clinic.

2. The rocket shot straight up and kept on going.

3. "Are the facts straight in your mind?" asked Gail.

4. "The lines on this page are not straight," the student complained.

Read these pairs of words with the class or the teacher.

Compare

am	aim		mad	maid
man	main		pad	paid
ran	rain		sad	said
pan	pain		lid	laid
plan	plain		chin	chain
bran	brain		ball	bail
clam	claim		fall	fail

The teacher will dictate 12 words.

1. _____

2. _____

3. _____

4. _____

5. _____

6. _____

7. _____

8. _____

9. _____

10. _____

11. _____

12. _____

Work with the teacher.

Use words from this box to complete the sentences below.

drain	laid	raise	sprain	straight	trail	train

1. When you fell, did you _____ your ankle?

2. The _____ to Main Street almost always departs on time.

3. Is the city going to _____ the fines on parking tickets?

4. Go _____ when you get to the stop sign on Holiday Drive.

5. The waitress _____ the menu on the table.

6. Was the _____ in the kitchen sink stopped up?

7. A hiker lost his way on a remote _____ in the Grand Canyon.

Make words with the **ai** vowel combination by using consonants. Write six words. The first one has been done for you.

_____brain_____

_____

_____

_____

_____

_____

Read with the teacher.

First pronounce all of these words after the teacher. The teacher will then pronounce one word in each row. Circle that word.

1. mail   mall   mile   mill

2. way   why   we   woe

3. pin   pine   pain   pan

4. tell   tall   tile   tail

5. sad   sod   side   said

6. wit   white   wait   what

7. rose   ruse   rise   raise

8. jail   gale   gal   jell

Join each word and its affix.

1. raise + ing = <u>   raising   </u>

2. ship + ed = <u>   </u>

3. brain + y = <u>   </u>

4. raisin + s = <u>   </u>

5. crab + y = <u>   </u>

6. sign + ing = <u>   </u>

7. trail + ed = <u>   </u>

8. smoke + y = <u>   </u>

9. wax + ed = <u>   </u>

10. grin + ing = <u>   </u>

Work with the teacher.

DICTIONARY PRONUNCIATION

First read the words in the list. Then, on the blank next to each phonetic spelling, write the correct word from the list. (Words will be left over.)

accept	agent	attic	absent
advise	aphid	apple	accent

1. attic ăt´ ĭk
2. ____________ ā´ jənt
3. ____________ ăb sənt
4. ____________ ăk sĭnt
5. ____________ ā´ fĭd
6. ____________ ăp əl

DIVIDE AND MARK

Divide each word into syllables and mark the vowels long (-) or short (˘). (Mark only the vowels that you hear.) The first one has been done for you.

1. halo hā lō
2. hello ____________
3. medic ____________
4. sunshine ____________
5. phono ____________
6. backbone ____________

WORD DICTATION

The teacher will dictate ten two-syllable words. One syllable has been given for each word. Write the missing syllable. Then write the whole word.

First Syllable	*Second Syllable*	*Word*
1. con	1. _____	1. _____
2. ex	2. _____	2. _____
3. im	3. _____	3. _____
4. pun	4. _____	4. _____
5. tran	5. _____	5. _____
6. _____	6. mit	6. _____
7. _____	7. nel	7. _____
8. _____	8. nic	8. _____
9. _____	9. clude	9. _____
10. _____	10. male	10. _____

Work with the teacher.

Read these two sentences.

1. People waited.

2. Twenty people waited by the main gate.

Sentence 1 is short while sentence 2 is much longer. These two sentences are printed in the grid on page 23.

Study the headings in the grid. Notice that both sentences in the grid have the same subject and the same verb. The subject *people* tells who. The verb *waited* tell what the people *did*.

In the longer sentence, the extra words give us **details**. They tell us *how many* people waited and *where* they waited.

Details are helpful but are not absolutely necessary. The subject and the verb *are* necessary.

Every sentence must have a subject and a verb.

Read sentences 3 to 8 out loud. Put two lines under the subject and one line under the verb. Insert each sentence into the grid on page 23. Be sure to ask yourself each question at the top of the grid. Sentences 1 and 2 have been done for you.

3. <u>Dogs</u> <u>ate</u>.

4. Some stray <u>dogs</u> <u>ate</u> the scraps.

5. Mr. Layton fixes old trucks on his days off.

6. My fist hit the tray with a bang.

7. Whales dive.

8. Ms. Raymond traveled to the city by train.

9.–10. Write two sentences of your own in the grid. (The verbs have been given.) Use the questions at the top of the grid. After you have written your sentences in the grid, copy them on the lines below the grid.

	SUBJECT	VERB	OBJECT			
Which? Whose? How Many?	Who? or What?	Does? Did? Will Do?	What? or Whom?	Where?	When? How Often? How Long?	How? Why?
1.	People	waited				
2. Twenty	people	waited		by the main gate		
3.						
4.						
5.						
6.						
7.						
8.						
9.		raises				
10.		fainted				

WORDS

_____   _____

_____   _____

_____   _____

_____   _____

_____   _____

_____   _____

_____   _____

_____   _____

_____   _____

_____

WORD GROUPS

_____

_____

_____

_____

_____

SENTENCES

_____

_____

_____

_____

_____

_____

The R-Controlled Vowels **or** and **ar**

Read with the teacher.

A vowel before an **r** is called an *r-controlled vowel*. The vowel is difficult to hear because you hear mainly the **r** sound. The /r/ *controls* the vowel sound.

You have studied words that contain **ar** in Student Book 1, Lesson 14. In words such as *car, farm, park,* and *hard,* the sound of the letter **a** is shown as /ä/. Now you will study words that contain **or**.

When **o** comes before **r**, it usually is pronounced /ȯ/, as in *north*. Most dictionaries show one dot over the **o** for this sound.

OR as in NORTH

Pronounce these words with the class or teacher.

or	north	sort	for	born
short	forty	corn	snort	form
horn	fork	storm	thorn	cork
horse	orange	stork		

Read these pairs of words with the class or teacher.

Compare

for	far
born	barn
form	farm
cord	card

Work with the teacher.

Complete each word by filling in the blank with **or** or **ar**.

1. n____th
2. c____
3. h____se
4. st____rt
5. c____n

6. st____m
7. ____ange
8. b____k
9. h____n
10. ____m

11. sh____t
12. d____k
13. f____k
14. h____m
15. th____rn

FOLLOWING DIRECTIONS

Below are three rows of words. Read them. Then, in each row, put a check after any word that has more letters than the first word in that row. The first one has been done for you.

1. acorn   forest ✓   storm
2. forty   absorb   normal
3. north   horse   form

Work with the teacher.

Read the sentences below. Each sentence contains an incorrect word. Cross out that word and write the correct word on the line.

1. Did you pay much ~~far~~ those shoes? _____for_____

2. The baby was barn on Thursday. _____

3. His wife barked a cake for the party. _____

4. Sing your name on the dotted line next to the red check mark._____

5. Gordon saddled his horse and rod into the forest. _____

6. Did you get your W-2 income tax farm?_____

Match each word in Column A with its definition in Column B. Write the letter of your answer on the line.

Column A	Column B
____ 1. chart	a. give up; abandon
____ 2. forgive	b. a market
____ 3. forty	c. a large insect that stings
____ 4. thorn	d. excuse; pardon
____ 5. carve	e. a strong, thick string; thin rope
____ 6. cord	f. 4×10
____ 7. mart	g. take in; soak up
____ 8. hornet	h. cut up
____ 9. absorb	i. a map or graph
____ 10. forsake	j. a sharp spike on the stem of a plant

Work with the teacher.

First pronounce these two-syllable words with your class or teacher.
Then divide each word with a slash (/).

1. morning _____

2. sorry _____

3. normal _____

4. forest _____

5. orphan _____

6. absorb _____

7. hornet _____

8. endorse _____

Put these words in alphabetical order.

forgot _____

normal _____

endorse _____

chart _____

orphan _____

forget _____

In each of the following groups of words, there is one that does not belong. Circle that word. Then, fill in the blank with another word that fits into the group. In the first row *hornet* is circled because it is the only word that does not belong to the mammal group. *Cat,* which *is* a mammal, is added in the blank.

1. horse	tiger	fox	(hornet)	dog	<u>cat</u>
2. grape	corn	apple	orange	plum	_____
3. shorts	pants	pens	shoes	socks	_____
4. stork	elm	pine	walnut	maple	_____
5. twenty	sixty	fourth	eighty	fifty	_____
6. Gordon	Ann	Nancy	Susan	Cathy	_____

OR as in WORK

Work with the teacher.

When **or** follows **w**, the **or** combination is pronounced as we hear it in *work*. Most dictionaries show this pronunciation as /ûr/.*

Pronounce these words with the class or teacher.

word	world	worse	worst
worry	worth	worm	worship

Make compound words.

1. work + shop = _____

2. worth + while = _____

3. world + wide = _____

*Two words are exceptions to the pronunciation rule: wore and worn.

PROVERBS

A proverb is a wise or well-known saying. It can be a true statement or can give advice or a warning. For example, the Golden Rule is a proverb. Read and discuss the Golden Rule.

Do unto others as you would have them do unto you.

Read these proverbs with the class or teacher. Discuss the meaning of each one.

1. His bark is worse than his bite.

2. Harsh words are hard to forget.

3. Worry is worse than hard work.

OR as in PORT

Work with the teacher.

In some or words, the **o** has a long **o** sound.

Dictionaries may show this sound as /ò/ or /ôr/.

Pronounce these words.

port	fort	pork	worn	story
sport	force	porch	sworn	glory

Read these sentences with the class or teacher.

1. A witness to the crime swore to tell the truth.

2. Old Glory is a nickname for the United States flag.

3. Four naval ships sailed into port last Tuesday morning.

4. A storm hit the Midwest with crushing force.

5. The tennis player had worn a hole in the sole of her left shoe.

A LANDLORD STORY

My landlord told me this story. He said that a stork landed in the parking lot the last time a baby was born here. The stork startled the dogs on the porch. Those dogs did not stop barking for forty days!

Read the above paragraph a second time and underline all words that contain the vowel combination **or**.

Work with the teacher.

First pronounce all of these words after the teacher. The teacher will then pronounce one word in each row. Circle that word.

1. bran   barn   brain

2. car   core   cure

3. word   world   ward

4. were   wore   war

5. from   form   frame

6. stroke   stork   struck

7. north   thorn   throne

8. tar   tire   tore

Join each word and its affix or affixes.

1. paint   +   ing   +   s   =   _____

2. for   +   give   +   ing   =   _____

3. bar   +   ed   =   _____

4. shine   +   y   =   _____

5. slop   +   ed   =   _____

6. slope   +   ed   =   _____

7. startle   +   ing   =   _____

8. orange   +   s   =   _____

9. worth   +   y   =   _____

10. morn   +   ing   =   _____

Work with the teacher.

DICTIONARY PRONUNCIATION

First read the words in the box. Then on the blank next to each phonetic spelling, write the correct word from that list. (Words will be left over.)

custom	cancel	central	carton	city
costume	cotton	carsick	crisis	cellar

1. _____ sĭt´ ē

2. _____ kăn´ səl

3. _____ sĕn´ trəl

4. _____ kăr´ tən

5. _____ kŏs´ toom

6. _____ sĕl´ ər

DIVIDE AND MARK

Divide each word into syllables and mark the vowels as either long or short. Place a long **e** above the **y** in words that end in **y**. The first two have been done for you.

1. tadpole   tăd pōle

2. study   stŭd ȳ

3. holly   _____

4. chastise   _____

5. phony   _____

6. insect   _____

WORD DICTATION

The teacher will dictate ten two-syllable words. One syllable has been given for each word. Write the missing syllable. Then write the whole word.

First Syllable	*Second Syllable*	*Word*
1. _____	1. ___gal___	1. _____
2. _____	2. ___nus___	2. _____
3. _____	3. ___pen___	3. _____
4. _____	4. ___ren___	4. _____
5. _____	5. ___val___	5. _____
6. _____	6. ___it___	6. _____
7. _____	7. ___on___	7. _____
8. _____	8. ___el___	8. _____
9. _____	9. ___im___	9. _____
10. _____	10. ___el___	10. _____

Work with the teacher.

You have learned that every sentence must have a *subject* and a *verb.* The subject tells who or what is doing the action. The verb tells the action.

A verb is a word such as *started,* which comes from the base verb *start.* Sometimes another word, called a **helping verb**, is used with the main verb. The helping verb comes first.

Examples: has started (The helping verb is *has.*)
are starting (The helping verb is *are.*)
will start (The helping verb is *will.*)

Notice that the main verb sometimes has an affix (**ed** or **ing**) and sometimes it does not.

Here is a list of common helping verbs:

am	was	do	have	can
are	were	does	has	may
is	did	will		

Each sentence below has two words that belong under the *verb* heading in the grid on page 38. Read the sentence out loud. Put two lines under the subject and one line under the verb. Then insert sentences into the grid. The first one has been done for you. Be sure to ask yourself each question at the top of the grid.

1. The traveling <u>salesman</u> <u>is</u> <u>paying</u> his hotel bill in the lobby now.

2. Gordon has endorsed the check.

3. The storm was moving to the north.

4. One workman can stack those boxes with a forklift.

5. I am buying a used car today.

6. His boss will send the report to Portland by Express Mail.

7. Four hens have laid seven eggs in the last two days.

8. Most students can pass the test by studying hard.

9.–10. Write two sentences of your own in the grid. (The verbs have been given.) Ask yourself each question at the top of the grid. After you have written your sentences in the grid, copy them on the lines below the grid.

Which? Whose? How Many?	SUBJECT	VERB	OBJECT			
	Who? or What?	Does? Did? Will Do?	What? or Whom?	Where?	When? How Often? How Long?	How? Why?
1. The traveling	salesman	is paying	his hotel bill	in the lobby	now	
2.						
3.						
4.						
5.						
6.						
7.						
8.						
9.		will scorch				
10.		is parking				

WORDS

_____	_____
_____	_____
_____	_____
_____	_____
_____	_____
_____	_____
_____	_____
_____	_____
_____	_____
_____	_____

WORD GROUPS

_____

_____

_____

_____

_____

_____

SENTENCES

_____

_____

_____

_____

_____

_____

The R-Controlled Vowels or and ar

Contractions

Read with the teacher.

The word *contraction* means *drawing together* or *shortening*. Many times, in bringing together two words we leave out some letters from one of the words. A new word formed in this way is called a *contraction*.

A contraction is usually made up of two words written as one. An *apostrophe* (') takes the place of the letter or letters that are left out.

Examples: he is   he is
                          he's (*contraction*)

                they are   they are
                          they're (*contraction*)

The first word in each contraction does not change. Only the second word will lose a letter.

Write a contraction using *is* for each combination.

1. he is   _____he's_____

2. she is   _____

3. it is   _____

4. there is   _____

5. that is   _____

6. who is   _____

7. what is   _____

8. where is   _____

In each of the above contractions, which letter is replaced by an apostrophe? ____

Work with the teacher.

Write the correct contraction in each blank. (Be sure to use a capital letter at the beginning of a sentence.) Then read the sentences with the class or teacher.

1. _____ that woman in the blue dress?
   (Who is)

2. _____ training the dogs not to bark at the mailman.
   (She is)

3. _____ almost time to harvest the corn.
   (It is)

4. _____ Mr. Taylor?
   (Where is)

5. _____ the best hotel in the city.
   (That is)

6. _____ helping Marcus paint the barn.
   (He is)

7. _____ the price of the car?
   (What is)

8. _____ on the desk in the den.
   (It is)

9. _____ a box of matches on the shelf.
   (There is)

10. _____ honking the horn?
    (Who is)

11. Call me if _____ a problem.
    (there is)

12. You can use the paint _____ in the shed.
    (that is)

Work with the teacher.

Write a contraction using *are* for each combination. Remember, the first word stays the same. Only the second word loses a letter. The first one has been done.

1. you are _____you're_____

2. we are _____

3. they are _____

In each contraction above, which letter is replaced by an apostrophe? ____

Rewrite each sentence using a contraction for the underlined words.

1. <u>You are</u> charging a lot on your credit card.   _____

2. <u>They are</u> taking that TV set to the dump.   _____

3. <u>We are</u> going to visit the dentist next Friday.   _____

HOMOPHONES

Compare these homophones. Discuss the meanings with the teacher.

they're   If they're coming, what time will they be here?
there   The files are there in the middle of the desk. There are two price tags on this scarf.

you're   You're blushing!
your   Your watch is on the coffee table.

Work with the teacher.

Write a contraction using *will* for each combination.*

1. I will   _____ I'll _____

2. you will   _____

3. he will   _____

4. she will   _____

5. it will   _____

6. we will   _____

7. they will   _____

In each contraction above, which letters are replaced by an apostrophe? ____

Add an apostrophe to the contraction in each sentence.

1. Ill call you at nine.

2. When the pilots go on strike, theyll walk the picket line.

3. Shell complain if I forget to call.

4. Do you think itll rain?

5. Well have a copy of the report by closing time.

6. I am sure youll like visiting Kansas City.

7. If your jacket gets wet, itll shrink.

*Note: *I shall* and *we shall* are not often used in Standard American English. The contractions for these combinations are the same as those for *I will* and *we will*.

Write a contraction using *have* for each combination. The first one has been done for you.

1. I have
$\qquad\qquad$ I've $\qquad\qquad$

2. you have
$\qquad\qquad\qquad\qquad$

3. we have
$\qquad\qquad\qquad\qquad$

4. they have
$\qquad\qquad\qquad\qquad$

5. must have
$\qquad\qquad\qquad\qquad$ *

In each contraction above, which letters are replaced by an apostrophe? ____

Fill in each blank. Write a contraction for the words that are given in parentheses. (Be sure to use capital letters where needed.) Then read the sentences with the class or teacher.

1. I think _____ had plenty of time to make up your mind.
(you have)

2. _____ lived in Salt Lake City since last March.
(we have)

3. Those shoes _____ cost a lot of money.
(must have)

4. _____ made all the plans for the Fourth of July parade.
(they have)

5. Mrs. Cain has no car. She _____ walked to work.
(must have)

6. We're bored, so _____ planned a party.
(we have)

7. _____ lost my glasses and cannot watch TV.
(I have)

8. _____ done a fine job scraping off the old paint.
(you have)

* This contraction is used when speaking but is almost never used in its written form.

Work with the teacher.

Write a contraction using *has* for each combination. The first one has been done for you.

1. he has   he's

2. she has   _____

3. it has   _____

In each of the above contractions, which letters are replaced by an apostrophe? ____

Use *has* with *he, she,* and *it.*

Example: She's waited all day for your phone call.
                 She has waited all day for your phone call.

Notice that the contractions for *has* and *is* are the same. The correct word is the one that makes sense in a sentence.

Examples: He's washing the car.
                 He is washing the car.
                 He's washed the car.
                 He has washed the car.

Rewrite each sentence. Write the two words that each contraction stands for.

1. That pipe is old, and *it has* become rusty.

_____

2. *She has* quit her job at the market.

_____

3. *He has* gone fishing.

_____

Work with the teacher.

Contractions can also be made with *names* of persons, places, and things.

Examples: <u>Jim is</u> working on a farm.
<u>Jim's</u> working on a farm.
<u>Jim has</u> worked on a farm since March.
<u>Jim's</u> worked on a farm since March.

Write the correct contraction in each blank. Then read the sentences with the class or teacher.

1. _____Jan's_____ moved to Memphis.
    (Jan has)

2. _____ the capital of the United States.
    (Washington is)

3. The _____ hiding under the sofa.
    (cat is)

4. _____ a nice time for a wedding.
    (June is)

5. The _____ on the table.
    (plate is)

6. _____ lost his wallet.
    (Mr. Morgan has)

7. The _____ cold and icy all of the time.
    (North Pole is)

8. The _____ ended.
    (war has)

9. _____ told that same joke five times.
    (Nick has)

10. The _____ lost her bottle.
    (baby has)

Work with the teacher.

Write a contraction using *had* for each combination.

1. I had   _____I'd_____

2. you had   _____

3. he had   _____

4. she had   _____

5. it had   _____

6. we had   _____

7. they had   _____

In each of the above contractions, which letters are replaced by an apostrophe? ____

Fill in each blank. Write the two words for which each contraction stands. (Be sure to use capital letters when needed.) Then read the sentences with the class or teacher.

1. _____ left work before the job was finished.
      (You'd)

2. By 10 P.M., _____ washed the dishes and mopped the kitchen.   (we'd)

3. _____ waxed the car by the time I got home.
      (She'd)

4. Until 1992, _____ always lived in Fort Worth.
        (they'd)

5. _____ gone to the store but forgot to buy ketchup.
    (He'd)

FOLLOWING DIRECTIONS

The word *among* means *somewhere in the group*. Among these words are some contractions.

Put a check before any word that is a contraction.

his	shed	were	you're	your
who's	there	well	whose	it'll
we'll	she's	wed	they'd	ill

OTHER COMMON CONTRACTIONS

Work with the teacher.

The word *am* is used with *I*. The **a** is left out of *am* in a contraction.

Examples: I'm not going to work today.
I am not going to work today.
I'm sure that you will pass the next test.
I am sure that you will pass the next test.

Another common contraction is let's. It stands for let us.

Examples: Let's order some pizza.
Let us order some pizza.
Let's go!
Let us go!

Study these contractions.

of the clock   o'clock

Madam   Ma'am

Hallowed (Holy)   Even (Evening)   Hallowed Even   Hallowe'en (This word is now usually spelled Halloween.)

Work with the teacher.

Write the correct contractions for each combination.

1. it is _____   7. she has _____

2. let us _____   8. I have _____

3. they are _____   9. madam _____

4. I had _____   10. we had _____

5. there is _____   11. you have _____

6. what is _____   12. of the clock _____

Write the two words for which each contraction stands.

1. you'll _____   6. it'll _____

2. we've _____   7. who's _____

3. that's _____   8. you're _____

4. I'm _____   9. where's _____

5. he's _____   10. let's _____

Read these pairs of words with the class or teacher.

Compare

we'll	well
we're	were
he'll	hell
she'll	shell
we'd	wed
she'd	shed
I'll	ill
he's	his

Work with the teacher.

First pronounce all of these words after the teacher. The teacher will then pronounce one word in each row. Circle that word.

1. we'll   well   will   whale

2. his   hiss   he's   has

3. shell   she'll   chill   shale

4. war   were   where   we're

5. I'll   ill   ail   all

6. shod   shad   she'd   shed

7. wad   we'd   wed   wade

8. I'd   aid   add   odd

Join each word and its affix.

1. fill   +   ed   = _____

2. file   +   ed   = _____

3. force   +   s   = _____

4. porch   +   s   = _____

5. wed   +   ing   = _____

6. use   +   ing   = _____

7. storm   +   y   = _____

8. shade   +   y   = _____

9. shag   +   y   = _____

10. rule   +   ing   = _____

Read with the teacher.

DICTIONARY PRONUNCIATION

Read the words in the list. On the blank next to each phonetic spelling, write the correct word from the list. (Words will be left over.)

garlic	gallon	jungle	gentle	gargle
jumbo	juggle	jello	jelly	garden

1. _____ jĕn´ təl

2. _____ gär´ dən

3. _____ jŭng´ gəl

4. _____ gär´ gəl

5. _____ jĕl´ ŏ

6. _____ găl´ lən

DIVIDE AND MARK

Divide each word into syllables and mark the vowels long, short, or schwa (ə). (Four words have a schwa in the second syllable.)

1. dental   ___dĕn´ təl___

2. bathtub   ___băth´ tŭb___

3. melon   _____

4. fatal   _____

5. cannot   _____

6. insane   _____

WORD DICTATION

The teacher will dictate ten two-syllable words. Write the missing syllable. Then write the whole word.

First Syllable	Second Syllable	Word
1. _____	1. ___cust___	1. _____
2. _____	2. ___lon___	2. _____
3. _____	3. ___it___	3. _____
4. _____	4. ___ment___	4. _____
5. _____	5. ___id___	5. _____
6. _____	6. ___in___	6. _____
7. _____	7. ___gan___	7. _____
8. _____	8. ___plex___	8. _____
9. _____	9. ___gent___	9. _____
10. _____	10. ___ven___	10. _____

SENTENCE FOCUS

Work with the teacher.

A *question* is a sentence that *asks* for information.

A question may begin with a helping verb. The subject will come between the helping verb and the main verb.

Example: Are (helping verb) you (subject) working (main verb) next Saturday?

In this sentence, the helping verb *are* comes first, then the subject *you*, and then the main verb *working*.

Each of the sentences below is a question and begins with one of these helping verbs: **am, is, are, have, will**.

Read each question out loud. Put one line under the main and helping verbs. Put two lines under the subject. The first two have been done.

1. <u>Are</u> <u>they</u> <u>raking</u> the yard?

2. <u>Will</u> <u>Marcus</u> <u>bring</u> his fishing rod?

3. Am I riding in your car?

4. Have they raised the flag?

5. Is Carl chopping logs for a fire?

6. Are you saving your money for a rainy day?

7. Will Margo miss the first inning?

8. Is she talking on the phone to Mr. Barton?

9. Have you paid the gas bill yet?

10. Am I taking the children in my van?

A question *asks* for information. A statement *gives* information.

Examples: Were the fish biting this morning? (Question)
                  The fish were biting this morning. (Statement)

Read each question out loud. Put two lines under the subject and one line under the helping and main verbs.

On the first line, change the question to a statement. On the second line, write the sentence again using a contraction. The first two have been done.

1. <u>Will</u> <u>she</u> <u>ask</u> the foreman for a job?

   <u>She will ask the foreman for a job.</u>

   <u>She'll ask the foreman for a job.</u>

2. <u>Am</u> <u>I</u> <u>supposed</u> to call the dentist?

   <u>I am supposed to call the dentist.</u>

   <u>I'm supposed to call the dentist.</u>

3. Are we taking the train?

   _____

   _____

4. Will he visit his uncle in Spain?

   _____

   _____

5. Have they paid for the tickets?

   _____

   _____

6. Is she putting garlic in the salad?

   _____

   _____

WORDS

_____ _____
_____ _____
_____ _____
_____ _____
_____ _____
_____ _____
_____ _____
_____ _____

WORD GROUPS

_____
_____
_____
_____
_____
_____

SENTENCES

_____
_____
_____
_____
_____
_____

Negative Contractions

Work with the teacher.

Negative means *no* or *not.*

A negative contraction is made from word combinations that contain *not.*

Examples: is not   isn't

             are not   aren't

The letter **o** is always left out in a negative contraction.

Write a negative contraction for each combination.

1. is not   _____isn't_____

2. are not   _____

3. was not   _____

4. were not   _____

5. have not   _____

6. has not   _____

7. had not   _____

8. did not   _____

9. does not   _____

10. must not   _____

In each contraction above, which letter is replaced by an apostrophe?
_____

THREE IRREGULAR NEGATIVE CONTRACTIONS

Work with the teacher.

Study these negative contractions.

cannot   can't

do not   don't (pronounced dōnt)

will not   won't (pronounced wōnt)

Write the correct negative contraction in each blank.

1. She _____won't_____ be at the clinic today. (will not)

2. Sam and Pete _____ (do not) like to drive those huge trucks.

3. Wiretapping _____ (is not) legal.

4. I _____ (have not) had time to do the wash.

5. Ms. Kent _____ (does not) live in Jackson.

6. The people on the late shift _____ (will not) start work until eleven o'clock.

7. Marge and Madge _____ (are not) twins.

8. You _____ (must not) park next to a fire hydrant.

9. Mr. Arden _____ (had not) told us that his party was postponed.

10. I'm sorry, but I _____ (cannot) get tickets to the All-Star game.

11. The Smiths _____ (will not) be here until six o'clock.

12. Some people _____ (do not) like pizza.

13. He _____ (was not) the man for that job.

14. My father _____ (has not) phoned me since last Tuesday.

15. We _____ (were not) home when the fire started.

16. Marcy _____ (did not) buy a Honda.

FOLLOWING DIRECTIONS

Work with the teacher.

In rows 1 and 2, put a check in front of any word that is *not* a contraction. The first row has been done for you. In row 3, put an **x** after any word that is a negative contraction. In row 4, put an **x** after any word that is not a negative contraction.

1. he'll   ✓shell   didn't   where's

2. they   hasn't   we've   your

3. didn't   she's   isn't   won't

4. who's   doesn't   I'll   they're

Work with the teacher.

Read these word groups with the class or teacher.

weren't in the graveyard on Hallowe'en

if the vampires don't bite

can't carve the pumpkin

doesn't like the witch costume

and won't be in the casket

hadn't fed the strange black cat

Cross out the letter or letters that are not used in a negative contraction.
Then write the contraction on the line.

Example: are n∅t _____aren't_____

1. does not   _____

2. had not   _____

3. did not   _____

4. cannot   _____

5. have not   _____

6. were not   _____

Write the two words for which each contraction stands.

1. wasn't   _____

2. aren't   _____

3. don't   _____

4. isn't   _____

5. hasn't   _____

6. won't   _____

Work with the teacher.

First pronounce all of these words after the teacher. The teacher will then pronounce one word in each row. Circle that word.

1. want   won't   went   when

2. don't   dent   dint   didn't

3. were   wire   we're   where

4. ail   vale   fail   they'll

5. has   haze   who's   hose

6. he'll   hill   who'll   hole

7. aim   I'm   am   an

8. we've   wave   whiff   wife

Join each word and its affix.

1. chase + ing = _____

2. nose + y = _____

3. hop + ed = _____

4. hope + ed = _____

5. quit + ing = _____

6. snap + y = _____

7. sort + ed = _____

8. beg + ed = _____

9. gripe + ing = _____

10. grip + ing = _____

Read with your teacher.

DICTIONARY PRONUNCIATION

Read the words in the box. On the blank next to each phonetic spelling, write the correct word from the list.

forgive	forecast	phonics	photo	forty
focus	phony	pony	forced	foxy

1. _____ fō′ nē

2. _____ fôr′ kăst

3. _____ fŏn′ ĭks

4. _____ fôrst′

5. _____ fō′ kəs

6. _____ fŏk′ sē

DIVIDE AND MARK

Divide each word into syllables and mark the vowels long, short, or schwa. (Four words have a schwa in the second syllable.)

1. canyon _____ căn´ yən _____

2. final _____ fī´ nəl _____

3. problem _____

4. hitchhike _____

5. gallon _____

6. jumbo _____

WORD DICTATION

The teacher will dictate ten two-syllable words. Write the missing syllable. Then write the whole word.

First Syllable	*Second Syllable*	*Word*
1. ___in___	1. _____	1. _____
2. ___dras___	2. _____	2. _____
3. ___hel___	3. _____	3. _____
4. ___can___	4. _____	4. _____
5. ___muf___	5. _____	5. _____
6. _____	6. ___tom___	6. _____
7. _____	7. ___tal___	7. _____
8. _____	8. ___net___	8. _____
9. _____	9. ___dom___	9. _____
10. _____	10. ___sil___	10. _____

Work with the teacher.

A *statement* is a sentence that *gives* information.

Example: The trains are running on time.

When a statement contains the word *not*, it is called a *negative statement.* The word *not* comes between the helping verb and the main verb.

Example: The trains are (helping verb) *not* running (main verb) on time.

Each of the sentences below is a negative statement and contains the word *not*. Read each sentence out loud. Put two lines under the subject. Circle the word *not* and put one line under the helping verb and the main verb. The first one has been done.

One of these helping verbs is used in each sentence: *were, do, does, did, has, can, may.*

1. You cannot force that mule to move.

2. That traffic signal does not change quickly.

3. Some students were not attending class.

4. I do not work on Sundays.

5. Mr. Clay did not forget the carton of milk.

6. The blue belt does not fit my waist.

7. That bondsman may not provide the bail.

8. The baby does not walk by herself yet.

9. Rain has not delayed the game.

10. A spark did not ignite the fire.

Read each sentence out loud. Put two lines under the subject and one line under the verb.

On the first line below each sentence, change the sentence to a *negative statement*. On the second line, write the sentence again using a *negative contraction*. The first two have been done.

1. The <u>pilot</u> <u>can</u> <u>fly</u> a jet.

   <u>The pilot cannot fly a jet.</u>

   <u>That pilot can't fly a jet.</u>

2. <u><u>They</u></u> <u>have fixed</u> the brakes on the Ford.

   <u>They have not fixed the brakes on the Ford.</u>

   <u>They haven't fixed the brakes on the Ford.</u>

3. We will finish this job by five o'clock.

   _____

   _____

4. Florence has signed the contract.

   _____

   _____

5. The judge is calling the bailiff.

   _____

   _____

6. One band was recording a song.

   _____

   _____

WORDS

_____   _____

_____   _____

_____   _____

_____   _____

_____   _____

_____   _____

_____   _____

_____   _____

_____   _____

WORD GROUPS

_____

_____

_____

_____

_____

_____

SENTENCES

_____

_____

_____

_____

_____

_____

Review

Work with the teacher.

Each word in Column A contains an affix. First, underline the affix. Then write the meaning of that affix on the line under Column B. Some affixes are used more than once.

Here is a list of affix meanings:

ed   past tense of a verb

ing   "doing" form of a verb

s   s form of a verb

s   more than one (plural)

y   *having* or *full of*

	Column A	Column B
____	1. sway<u>s</u>	<u>s form of a verb</u>
____	2. fainting	_____
____	3. stormy	_____
____	4. waited	_____
____	5. barns	_____
____	6. spraying	_____
____	7. thorny	_____
____	8. prays	_____

Write the abbreviation for each day of the week.

Sunday _____   Wednesday _____   Saturday _____

Monday _____   Thursday _____

Tuesday _____   Friday   _____

SPELLING THE LONG SOUND OF A

Work with the teacher.

So far you have learned four ways to spell /a/.

Key Word	Spelling
SAFE	**a** with a silent **e** at the end of the word
BACON	**a** at the end of an open syllable
DAY	**ay** combination
RAIN	**ai** combination

Read this paragraph.

Most frogs lay eggs in water. A baby frog hatches from the egg as a tadpole. It begins life with gills and a tail. In time, the gills and tail are replaced by four legs. The frog is then able to live on land.

In the paragraph above, underline the six words that contain the long sound of the letter **a**.

Write the correct contraction for each combination.

1. have not   _____

2. they are   _____

3. it is   _____

4. will not   _____

5. you have   _____

6. cannot   _____

7. they had   _____

8. do not   _____

9. I am   _____

10. he will   _____

11. are not   _____

12. we are   _____

Work with the teacher.

The subject of a sentence tells *who* or *what* did the action. The verb tells what the subject *did* or *does*. Read these sentences. Put two lines under the subject and one line under the verb.

1. The judge praised the jury.

2. Snails invaded my yard last spring.

3. That landlady collects the rent by mail.

A verb is a word or word group that expresses action. In each of these sentences the verb is made up of two words, the helping verb and the main verb. Find the main verb and underline it. Then circle the helping verb.

1. Some horses were grazing.

2. Mr. Clark will sign the contract.

3. Ms. Harmon is arriving today.

Change each question into a statement.

1. Was Mrs. York working at the diner?

   _____

2. Will that ship sail in a short time?

   _____

Change each sentence into a negative statement by adding the word *not*.

1. His granddad was telling a story.

   _____

2. The sale will start on Friday.

   _____

Lesson 6

The Schwa **a** as an Open Syllable

Read with the teacher.

You have learned that an open syllable ends with a vowel. The vowel in an open syllable usually has a long sound, as in these words:

April   h**u**man   mott**o**

In some words, however, the vowel in an open syllable has a *schwa* sound. For example, many two-syllable words begin with the letter **a**. The **a** by itself is an open syllable but does not have a long sound. It has a schwa sound.

Example: alone   ǝ lone

Follow these instructions:

1. Pronounce the words below with the class or teacher. Then divide each word into syllables. The first syllable will be *open* with the schwa sound.

2. Place the schwa symbol (ə) over each beginning **a**.

3. Mark the vowel in the second syllable as long (ˉ) or short (˘). (Mark only the vowels that you *hear*.)

1. amaze   _ə̄ mā̄ze′_

2. alive   _____

3. ago   _____

4. adult   _____

5. amend   _____

6. adopt   _____

THE BEGINNING AFFIX A

Work with the teacher.

The schwa **a** at the beginning of a word usually is an affix. It has several meanings, but most often it means *on, to, in,* or *for.*

Examples: ashore   on shore

                     await   to wait for

                     abed   in bed

                     awhile   for a while

Join each root word and its affixes.

1. a + shame + ed = _____

2. a + rise + ing = _____

3. a + wait + ing = _____

4. a + mend + ed = _____

5. a + wake + ing = _____

Match each word in Column A with its definition in Column B. Write the letter of your answer on the line.

Column A   *Column B*

____ 1. alive   **a.** past tense of arise

____ 2. afire   **b.** to rise; to get up

____ 3. arise   **c.** in the past; gone by

____ 4. amend   **d.** having life

____ 5. aside   **e.** on fire

____ 6. adrift   **f.** to change; to correct; to add to

____ 7. ago   **g.** drifting

____ 8. arose   **h.** on the side; to one side

Read with the teacher.

Almost all two-syllable English words have one *strong* syllable and one *weak* syllable. Most dictionaries show an *accent mark* after the *strong* syllable. If you look up the word *adopt* in the dictionary to check to pronunciation, you will find

adopt (ə dŏpt´)

You can tell that the second syllable is the strong syllable because it has an accent mark after it. *

The first syllable in the word *adopt* is shown as a schwa. It is the *weak* syllable, so it has no mark after it.[†]

Follow these instructions.

1. Each of the following words begins with a schwa **a**. Divide each word into syllables. The first syllable will be *open* with a schwa sound.

2. Place the schwa symbol (ə) over each beginning **a**.

3. Mark the vowel in the second syllable long (‑) or short (˘). (Mark only the vowels that you *hear*.)

4. Place an *accent mark* at the end of the second syllable. The first one has been done for you.

1. alike ə̆ līk´	**4.** awhile _____	**7.** adrift _____
2. adapt _____	**5.** alone _____	**8.** awake _____
3. abuse _____	**6.** amuse _____	

*Strong syllables are called accented or stressed syllables.
†Weak syllables are called unaccented or unstressed syllables.

Work with the teacher.

MAVERICKS: *Study these sight words with the teacher.*

again against

Write the *pronunciation* of each of these words. Use the dictionary.

1. again _____   **2.** against _____

Read these words with the class or teacher.

ablaze	adore	against
abridge	adult	ago
abrupt	afire	ajar
acute	aflame	alarm
adapt	afraid	alike
adopt	again	aline (or align)
alive	amuse	astray
alone	apart	await
along	arise	awake
amaze	arose	award
amend	ashore	away
amid	aside	awhile

Read these sentences with the class or teacher. Circle each word that begins with the schwa **a.**

1. A cargo ship docked alongside the wharf.

2. Forty people went ashore.

3. "Don't go yet," her grandchild begged. "Stay awhile!"

4. Do you have a smoke alarm in your home?

5. Children often are afraid of the dark.

6. The plane was aloft by the time the rainstorm started.

THE AFFIX MENT

Read with the teacher.

The affix **ment** can be added to some words that begin with the schwa **a.** This ending affix means *the act of* and is pronounced /mənt/.

Join each word and its ending affix. Do not drop the silent **e** in the root word when you add **ment.** (Remember, you drop the silent **e** only when an affix begins with a vowel.)

1. amaze   +   ment   =   _____

2. amend   +   ment   =   _____

3. apart   +   ment   =   _____

4. amuse   +   ment   =   _____

5. agree   +   ment   =   _____

The teacher will dictate eight words. The first syllable, which is a schwa **a** in all of the words, is done for you. Write the second syllable on the line. Then write the whole word.

1. a _____   _____

2. a _____   _____

3. a _____   _____

4. a _____   _____

5. a _____   _____

6. a _____   _____

7. a _____   _____

8. a _____   _____

The Schwa a as an Open Syllable

Read with the teacher.

Some words end with the letter **a**. The **a** in these words has a schwa sound. It is an *open* syllable.

Follow these instructions.

1. Pronounce these words with the class or teacher. Then divide the words into syllables. The first syllable in each word may be *open* or *closed.*

2. Mark the vowel in the first syllable as long (ˉ) or as short (˘).

3. The second syllable in each word ends with the letter **a**. The **a** has the schwa sound. Place the schwa symbol (ə) over each ending **a**.

4. Place an accent mark at the end of the strong syllable. Remember, you will never find a schwa in a strong syllable. The first one has been done for you.

1. soda ___sō′___ ___da (ə)___

2. tuna ________ ________

3. extra ________ ________

4. sofa ________ ________

5. data ________ ________

6. coma ________ ________

7. comma ________ ________

8. hula ________ ________

9. panda ________ ________

10. nova ________ ________

The names of places are usually given in a special section in the back of a dictionary. The section is called *Persons and Places* or *Geographical Names* or *Gazetteer*. Look up these places in the dictionary. Tell what they are and where they are located. Can you locate them on a map?

1. Tampa _____

2. Yuma _____

3. Tulsa _____

Read with the teacher.

Many names of women end with the schwa **a** sound. In each name below, the vowel in the *first* syllable will be long or short. The vowel in the *second* syllable will have a schwa sound.

Follow these instructions.

1. Put the names in alphabetical order.

2. Divide the names into syllables.

3. Mark the vowel in the first syllable long (‑) or short (˘) and the **a** in the second syllable schwa (ə).

Name	Alphabetical Order	Syllables	
1. Lola	Brenda	Brĕn´	dặ
2. Sandra	_____	_____	_____
3. Donna	_____	_____	_____
4. Brenda	_____	_____	_____
5. Greta	_____	_____	_____
6. Rosa	_____	_____	_____
7. Linda	_____	_____	_____

Read these sentences with the class or teacher. Look at the beginning and the end of each sentence. Something is wrong or missing. Make the corrections. The first one has been done.

1. Is China the home of the panda?

2. he studying data processing

3. did you buy some extra soda for the picnic

4. where is Cuba

Read this passage with the teacher.

FAME

Fame makes some of us want to hide. Greta Garbo was a fine film actress. Her fans adored her, but she hid from them. She did not like to be in the public eye. In fact, the press called her a recluse. It was Garbo who said, "I want to be alone."

Work with the teacher.

Three of the two-syllable words in the above passage contain an **a** that has a schwa sound. Underline those three words.

Discuss the meaning of this sentence:

She did not like to be in the public eye.

FOLLOWING DIRECTIONS

Cross out any word that does not begin with schwa **a**. The first row has been done.

adult	gr~~a~~in	awhile	so~~f~~a	car~~g~~o
comma	ago	horse	awake	apartment
against	office	tuna	strain	away
world	don't	afraid	glory	panda

PHONICS REVIEW

Work with the teacher.

First pronounce all of these words after the teacher. Then the teacher will pronounce one word in each row. Listen, then circle that word.

1. along   alone   aline

2. afraid   afar   afire

3. await   away   awake

4. coma   come   comma

5. amuse   amaze   amass

6. abide   abate   abet

7. adopt   adapt   adept

8. tune   tundra   tuna

Join each word and its affix or affixes.

1. a + part + ment = _____

2. pet + ing = _____

3. craze + y = _____

4. skid + ed = _____

5. ail + ment = _____

6. age + ing = _____

7. handle + ed = _____

8. star + y = _____

9. pay + ment = _____

10. a + maze + ing = _____

Read with the teacher.

DICTIONARY PRONUNCIATION

Read the words in the box. On the blank next to each phonetic spelling, write the correct word from the list.

until	awake	away	under	unite
ugly	again	afraid	unit	await

1. _____ ŭg´ lē

2. _____ yōō´ nĭt

3. _____ ə wā´

4. _____ ə wāt´

5. _____ ə gĭn´

6. _____ ŭn´ dər

DIVIDE AND MARK

You will find a schwa **a** in each of these words. Divide each word and mark the vowels. Then add an accent mark after the *strong* syllable. Remember, a syllable with a schwa is never the strong syllable. The first two have been done for you.

1. awoke   _____ə wōk′_____

2. Tulsa   _____Tŭl′ sə_____

3. ablaze   _____

4. China   _____

5. abet   _____

6. under   _____

WORD DICTATION

The teacher will dictate ten two-syllable words. Write the missing syllable. Then write the whole word.

First Syllable	Second Syllable	Word
1. _____	1. ___ty___	1. _____
2. _____	2. ___y___	2. _____
3. _____	3. ___dy___	3. _____
4. _____	4. ___ny___	4. _____
5. _____	5. ___y___	5. _____
6. ___gra___	6. _____	6. _____
7. ___sen___	7. _____	7. _____
8. ___fan___	8. _____	8. _____
9. ___ho___	9. _____	9. _____
10. ___la___	10. _____	10. _____

SENTENCE FOCUS

Work with the teacher.

You have learned that every sentence must have a subject and a verb. Many sentences also need an *object* to *complete the action.*

Example: Mr. Mota is renting an apartment in Tulsa.

The subject *Mr. Mota* tells *who* is doing the action. The verb *is renting* tells the action.

The word *apartment* is the *object* of the verb because it tells *what* Mr. Mota is renting. It completes the action.

Read the first six sentences out loud. Notice that each of these sentences has an *object*. Put two lines under the subject and one line under the verb.

Insert each sentence into the grid on page 92. Ask yourself each question at the top of the grid. The first two have been done.

1. <u>Donna</u> <u>was watering</u> the grapevine with a long hose.

2. A <u>typist</u> <u>can finish</u> those letters alone.

3. The Harmons adopted an orphan last spring.

4. Linda put the cans on the shelf.

5. Some trucks will dump sand on the highway in a little while.

6. The small girl can set the alarm by herself.

Fill in the blanks with an object for each sentence below. Put two lines under the subject and one line under the verb. Then insert the sentences into the grid. Use the questions at the top of the grid.

7. The comic amuses _____ with his jokes.

8. A waiter was putting _____ on the table.

9. Some adults will take the _____ to the ball park.

10. Carla is stuffing _____ in her pockets.

11. Mr. Martin got a _____ at the lab last Thursday.

12. Mona has locked the _____ with a padlock.

Which? Whose? How Many?	SUBJECT	VERB	OBJECT			
	Who? or What?	Does? Did? Will Do?	What? or Whom?	Where?	When? How Often? How Long?	How? Why?
1.	Donna	was watering	the grapevine			with a long hose
2.	A typist	can finish	those letters			alone
3.						
4.						
5.						
6.						
7.						
8.						
9.						
10.						
11.						
12.						

WORDS

_____   _____
_____   _____
_____   _____
_____   _____
_____   _____
_____   _____
_____   _____
_____   _____
_____   _____

WORD GROUPS

_____
_____
_____
_____
_____

SENTENCES

_____
_____
_____

The Three /ûr/s—**er**, **ir**, and **ur**

Read with the teacher.

Three r-controlled combinations have the same sound.

er as in clerk

ir as in girl

ur as in nurse

Most dictionaries show this pronunciation as /ûr/.

The r-controlled vowel was discussed in Lesson 2. A vowel before an r is difficult to hear because you mainly hear the **r** sound. The /r/ controls the vowel sound.

It is much easier to read words with **er, ir,** and **ur** than it is to spell them. In spelling, the choice can be difficult. How can you remember that the word *nerve* is spelled with **er** and not as "nirve" or "nurve"?

By practicing the spelling of these words in easy steps as you go through this book, you will begin to build a visual memory for these three /ûr/s.

The first combination you will study is **er: er** as in clerk.

Pronounce these words with the class or teacher.

her	clerk	perch
germ	jerk	merge
term	nerve	verge
fern	swerve	verse

Work with the teacher.

Write these words in alphabetical order.

perch   _____

germ   _____

nerve   _____

fern   _____

her   _____

term   _____

swerve   _____

merge   _____

Pronounce these words and then answer the questions below.

germ	jerk	port	merge
card	term	clerk	worry

1. Which two words rhyme with *work*? _____ and _____

2. Which word rhymes with *verge*? _____

3. Which two words rhyme with *worm*? _____ and _____

Look up the name of the place listed below and answer the questions. Although this name may be listed in the regular section of the dictionary, some dictionaries will list it in a special section at the back.

Alberta

1. Write the pronunciation. _____

2. What is it? _____

3. In which part of the dictionary did you find it? _____

Work with the teacher.

Divide these words into syllables.

1. person   _____per_____   _____son_____

2. serpent   _____   _____

3. alert   _____   _____

4. sermon   _____   _____

5. western   _____   _____

6. vermin   _____   _____

7. percent   _____   _____

8. northern   _____   _____

9. hermit   _____   _____

10. perhaps   _____   _____

Fill in the missing letters to make a word that matches the definition. Choose a word from the list on page 96.

1. A man, woman, or child   _____ *per* _____son

2. Maybe   _____haps

3. One of a hundred parts   _____cent

4. Wide awake; watchful   a_____

5. From the north   north _____

6. Bugs, lice, rats, mice   _____min

7. A person who lives alone, far away from people
    _____mit

8. A snake   _____pent

9. A long, serious talk or speech   _____mon

10. From the west   west_____

MAVERICKS: *Study these sight words with the teacher.*

danger	**dangerous**

Read the sentences with the class or teacher.

1. Icebergs are a danger to ships.

2. Red Cross workers went into a dangerous zone.

3. A sign was posted that said, DANGER—DO NOT ENTER.

Work with the teacher.

Hundreds of English words end in **er**. At the end of a two- or three-syllable word, **er** usually is an unstressed syllable. This unaccented syllable is shown in dictionaries as *schwa r*, pronounced /ər/. Pronounce these words with the class or teacher. Be careful! Most of the *first* syllables in the words are closed, although some are open.

batter	supper	cider	enter
better	dinner	spider	after
bitter	summer	sister	rafter
butter	winter	blister	center
master	ladder	paper	tamper
mister	later	pepper	temper
plaster	letter	partner	thunder
blister	litter	pamper	tender
ever	matter	sober	slander
never	meter	slipper	slender
lever	bitter	salver	banner
clever	mutter	silver	fender
over	member	order	river
under	number	border	rubber
clover	manner	gather	clatter
blunder	monster	rather	clutter
whisper	lumber	timber	liver
whisker	slumber	limber	sliver
whimper	shelter	glimmer	quiver
wicker	swelter	shimmer	shiver

September	remember	carpenter	cylinder
October	contender	register	lavender
November	semester	minister	passenger
December	protester	sinister	messenger

Work with the teacher.

MAVERICKS: Study these sight words with the teacher.

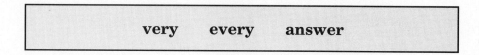

very   every   answer

Read these word groups with the class or teacher.

had a very dangerous job

perhaps the answer is

on the twenty-fifth of every December

where the two rivers merge

was on the verge of crying

doesn't have the nerve

along the western ridge of the hill

got rid of all the vermin and germs

The teacher will dictate 14 words from the long list of words ending in **er** given on pages 98–99. After the dictation:

1. Divide each word into syllables.

2. Put an accent over the strongest syllable.

3. Mark the vowel in the strongest syllable as long or short.

4. Put the schwa r symbol, ər, over the proper syllable.

1. _____

2. _____

3. _____

4. _____

5. _____

6. _____

7. _____

8. _____

9. _____

10. _____

11. _____

12. _____

13. _____

14. _____

Work with the teacher.

Pronounce these words with the class or teacher. Then copy the words in the blanks below the box.

sir	girl	dirt	firm	third
stir	twirl	shirt	squirm	thirty
bird	shirl	skirt	first	irk
birth	swirl	squirt	thirst	smirk

____ ____ ____ ____ ____

____ ____ ____ ____ ____

____ ____ ____ ____ ____

____ ____ ____ ____ ____

Read this paragraph with the class or teacher. Then answer the questions below.

DUST DEVIL

A whirlwind is a strong, whirling mass of wind. An intense whirlwind may be as big as a cyclone or tornado. A small whirlwind is called a *dust devil*. A dust devil happens in the desert on hot, calm days. As it rises, a dust devil sucks up sand in a sudden, swirling rush.

1. What is a dust devil? _____

2. Where do you find it? _____

3. When does it happen? _____

Work with the teacher.

Divide these words into syllables with a slash (/).

1. skirmish   skir/mish

2. birthday   _____

3. whirlwind   _____

4. circle   _____

5. circus   _____

6. stirrup   _____

7. circus   _____

8. squirrel   _____

Draw a line between word groups in Column A and Column B to form complete sentences.

Column A	Column B
1. Ms. Kird works for	on the first Monday of September.
2. That black car	with a circus.
3. Is her birthday	has circled the block six times.
4. Labor Day falls	the third of October?
5. He is a trapeze artist	by registered mail?
6. Were those letters sent	a legal firm.

Complete each word with the letters **ir** or **er**. The first one has been done for you.

1. f_ir_st   6. sh____t

2. th____d   7. cl___k

3. h____   8. n___ve

4. g____m   9. d___t

5. g____l

Make words with the *ir* combination by putting letters before and after it. Your words can have as many syllables as you like. The first word has been done for you.

Write six words.

_____thirst_____

_____

_____

_____

_____

_____

FOLLOWING DIRECTIONS

Read with the teacher.

You have learned that a sight word is a word that is not spelled the way it sounds.

Among the words below, you will find four sight words. Put a circle around each one.

spider	fern	shirt	every
flirt	very	circus	thunder
answer	germ	blister	danger

PROVERBS

Read these proverbs with the class or teacher. Discuss the meaning of each.

1. All that glitters is not gold.

2. Cast no dirt into the well that gives you water.

3. Don't cry over spilled milk.

4. A bird in the hand is worth two in the bush.

The teacher will dictate 20 words from any of the schwa **er** words that have appeared in the lesson so far (or any others the teacher chooses).

1. _____	6. _____	11. _____	16. _____
2. _____	7. _____	12. _____	17. _____
3. _____	8. _____	13. _____	18. _____
4. _____	9. _____	14. _____	19. _____
5. _____	10. _____	15. _____	20. _____

Work with the teacher.

Pronounce these words with the class or teacher. Then copy the words in the blanks below the box.

nurse	hurt	urge
purse	church	curb
burn	burst	curve
turn	surf	curl

_____   _____   _____

_____   _____   _____

_____   _____   _____

_____   _____   _____

First pronounce the words in the box below. Then choose a word from the box that matches a definition below. Fill in the missing letters to complete each word.

current	furnish	pursue	suburb	urban
disturb	murmur	Saturn	survive	urgent

1. Up-to-date; at the present time _____ rent

2. To supply; to provide; to equip _____nish

3. Related to a city; having to do with _____ban

4. The second largest planet of the solar system
   Sat_____

5. To stay alive _____vive

6. To upset; to interfere with dis _____

7. Important; pressing _____gent

8. To chase; to go after _____sue

9. A district or small city close to a large city sub_____

10. To talk very softly _____ _____

Divide these words into syllables.

1. surprise _____   _____

2. surplus _____   _____

3. hurry _____   _____

4. Thursday _____   _____

5. purple _____   _____

6. sturdy _____   _____

7. further _____   _____

8. murder _____   _____

9. turtle _____   _____

10. turkey _____   _____

Read this paragraph with the class or teacher.

FOUR DAYS OF HARD LUCK

On Thursday, Shirley burned her arm. On Friday, it still hurt. On Saturday, she ripped her shirt. On Sunday, she was in a hurry and went to church in a dirty skirt.

Read the paragraph again and underline the 12 words that contain the sound of /ûr/.

Make words with the **ûr** sound by putting letters before and after it. Remember that this sound can be spelled with *er* and *ir* as well as *ur.*

Write six words.

_____ _____

_____ _____

_____ _____

Work with the teacher.

Read these sentences with the class or teacher.

1. Carpenters returned the surplus lumber after they finished the job.

2. Ninety-six passengers survived the plane crash.

3. "You can make a U-Turn at the corner," the officer told the driver. "Then park next to the curb."

4. Thanksgiving falls on the fourth Thursday of November.

5. Every day, I'm getting further behind in my work.

6. "Where's Dr. Herman?" murmured a timid clerk. "He has an urgent phone call."

7. A sharp curve at the end of Churchill Drive is very dangerous.

8. "Where does it hurt?" a nurse asked the sobbing child.

9. The woman surprised the purse snatcher by punching him in the ribs.

10. A moment after impact, the truck burst into flames.

11. The sturdy old table was marred with scratches and burn marks.

12. The word *hamburger* is named after Hamburg, a city in Germany.

The teacher will dictate twelve words containing the **ûr** or ər sounds from among those in word lists or sentences used so far in the lesson (or other words of the teacher's choice).

1. _____   7. _____

2. _____   8. _____

3. _____   9. _____

4. _____   10. _____

5. _____   11. _____

6. _____   12. _____

PHONICS REVIEW

Work with the teacher.

First pronounce all of these words after the teacher. The teacher will then pronounce one word in each row.

1. bitter   butter   batter   better

2. shirk   jerk   shirt   skirt

3. frame   fame   farm   firm

4. piper   paper   pepper   popper

5. wore   war   where   were

6. burn   bran   barn   brain

7. fare   fur   fire   far

8. cave   crave   carve   curve

Join each word and its affix.

1. stir   + ed   = _____

2. circle   + ing   = _____

3. merge   + ed   = _____

4. blur   + ed   = _____

5. dirt   + y   = _____

6. nerve   + s   = _____

7. urge   + ing   = _____

8. fur   + y   = _____

9. thirst   + y   = _____

10. survive   + ed   = _____

Work with the teacher.

DICTIONARY PRONUNCIATION

Read the words in the box. On the blank next to each phonetic spelling, write the correct word from the box.

thunder	thirst	Thursday	turkey	turnip
turtle	thrust	turnpike	timber	thirty

1. _____ tûrn´ pīk

2. _____ tûr´ təl

3. _____ thûr´ tē

4. _____ thûrz´ dā

5. _____ tûr´ kē

6. _____ tûr´ nĭp

DIVIDE AND MARK

Each of these words has a schwa sound in one of the syllables. Divide each word and mark the vowels. Then add an accent mark after the *strong* syllable. Remember, a syllable with a schwa is never the strong syllable.

1. arose _____ ə rōs´ _____

2. vocal _____ vō´ cəl _____

3. agog _____

4. census _____

5. amid _____

6. slogan _____

WORD DICTATION

The teacher will dictate ten two-syllable words. Write the missing syllable. Then write the whole word.

First Syllable	Second Syllable	Word
1. _____	1. ____lo____	1. _____
2. _____	2. ____bo____	2. _____
3. _____	3. ____go____	3. _____
4. _____	4. ____to____	4. _____
5. _____	5. ____to____	5. _____
6. ____ve____	6. _____	6. _____
7. ____mem____	7. _____	7. _____
8. ____po____	8. _____	8. _____
9. ____tem____	9. _____	9. _____
10. ____so____	10. _____	10. _____

The Three /ûr/s—er, ir, and ur

Work with the teacher.

Read each sentence out loud. Put two lines under the subject and one line under the verb.

Insert the sentences into the grid on the next page. Ask yourself each question listed at the top of the grid.

Note that *How Often?* and *How Long?* have been added under the heading *When?*

1. <u>Mr. Sherman</u> <u>shaves</u> every morning (*how often*) with a straight razor.

2. <u>Kirsten</u> <u>can watch</u> the children until nine o'clock (*how long*).

3. This stone church will remain here for a long time.

4. Some birds migrate north every spring.

5. The bell will ring for 30 seconds.

6. A salesclerk has put my jacket in layaway until payday.

7. Somebody collects the mail twice a day.

8. Ms. Burns drinks nonfat milk most of the time.

9.–10. Write two sentences of your own in the grid. The verbs have been given. Use the questions at the top of the grid. Then copy your sentences on the lines below the grid.

Which? Whose? How Many?	SUBJECT	VERB	OBJECT			
	Who? or What?	Does? Did? Will Do?	What? or Whom?	Where?	When? How Often? How Long?	How? Why?
1.	Mr. Sherman	shaves			every morning	with a straight razor
2.	Kirsten	can watch	the children		until nine o'clock	
3.						
4.						
5.						
6.						
7.						
8.						
9.		will return				
10.		paid				

WORDS

_____   _____

_____   _____

_____   _____

_____   _____

_____   _____

_____   _____

_____   _____

_____   _____

WORD GROUPS

_____

_____

_____

_____

_____

_____

SENTENCES

_____

_____

_____

_____

_____

_____

The Affixes **er** and **est**

Read with the teacher.

At the end of a root word, the affix **er** has one of three meanings:

1. a person who

Example: drive + er = driver (a person who drives)

2. a thing that

Example: wash + er = washer (a thing that washes)

3. more

Example: hot + er = hotter (more hot)

This third meaning is very different from the first two meanings.

Reminder: The Doubling Rule

In English, a vowel in a one-syllable word will be long if it is separated from a final vowel by a single consonant.

Example: hate = hāt
cape = cāp
rate = rāt
tape = tāp

Without the final vowel after the final single consonant, the main vowel sound of a single-syllable word will have a short sound.

hat = hăt
cap = căp
rat = răt
tap = tăp

This means that if you add an *er* or *est* ending to words with short vowels and single final consonants, you will make the main vowel long. So when you see a single-syllable word with a short vowel that ends with a single consonant, double the final consonant before adding an ending like *er, est,* or *ing.*

THE AFFIX ER—A PERSON WHO

Join each root word and its affix.

1. swim + er = _____swimmer_____ (a person who swims)

2. vote + er = _____ (a person who votes)

3. sing + er = _____ (a person who sings)

4. love + er = _____ (a person who loves)

5. weld + er = _____ (a person who welds)

6. jog + er = _____ (a person who jogs)

Fill in each blank with the correct word.

1. The man farms. He is a _____farmer_____.

2. Ms. Marner rents an apartment. She is a _____.

3. Jesse James robbed trains. He was a train _____.

4. Some people shop a lot. They are _____.

5. Val makes a living taking photographs. She is a _____.

6. Those men explored places. They were _____.

Work with the teacher.

Join each root word and its affix.

1. mix   +   er   =   _____mixer_____ (a thing that mixes)

2. lock   +   er   =   _____ (a thing that locks)

3. glide   +   er   =   _____ (a thing that glides)

4. zip   +   er   =   _____ (a thing that zips)

5. buzz   +   er   =   _____ (a thing that buzzes)

6. fold   +   er   =   _____ (a thing that folds)

7. slice   +   er   =   _____ (a thing that slices)

Fill in each blank with the correct word.

1. A turkey gobbles. It is a _____*gobbler*_____.

2. That gadget opens cans. It is a can _____.

3. The turn signal on a car blinks. Sometimes it is called a

_____.

4. The student must erase a word. She needs an _____.

5. This gummed label sticks on things. It is a _____.

6. That device makes coffee. It is a coffee _____.

7. The clerk will staple those papers. He will use a _____.

Write the root word and its affix.

1. _____dip_____ + _____er_____ = dipper

2. _____ + _____ = rocker

3. _____ + _____ = trimmer

4. _____ + _____ = bumper

5. _____ + _____ = timer

Read with the teacher.

Dividing words into syllables may be different than dividing words into roots and affixes.

Example: hunter
               hun ter   Divided by syllables
               hunt er   Divided by root word and affix

Syllables help you to pronounce and spell a word by dividing it into small parts:

               hun ter   Divided by syllables

A root word and its affix helps you to understand the meanings of the word parts:

               hunt er   One who hunts

Sometimes, dividing a word into syllables may be the same as dividing it by root and affix.

Example: hanger
               hang er   Divided by syllables
               hang er   Divided by root word and affix, A thing that hangs

Divide these words into *syllables*.

Root Word	Affix		Word	Divide the Word into Syllables	
1. bake	+ er	=	baker	_____	_____
2. start	+ er	=	starter	_____	_____
3. sing	+ er	=	singer	_____	_____
4. sift	+ er	=	sifter	_____	_____
5. burn	+ er	=	burner	_____	_____

THE AFFIX ER—MORE

Work with the teacher.

Join each root word and its affix.

1. wise + er = _____wiser_____ (more wise)

2. sad + er = _____ (more sad)

3. large + er = _____ (more large)

4. tame + er = _____ (more tame)

5. sharp + er = _____ (more sharp)

Write the root word and its affix.

1. ____mad____ + ____er____ = madder

2. ____late____ + ____er____ = later

3. _____ + _____ = richer

4. _____ + _____ = hotter

5. _____ + _____ = stronger

6. _____ + _____ = nicer

The **er** affix in the word *pitcher* means *a person who* (a person who pitches).

The **er** affix in the word *mixer* means *a thing that* (a thing that mixes).

The **er** affix in the word **fresher** means *more* (more fresh).

Answer the questions below. Choose from one of these definitions:

1. a person who   **2.** a thing that   **3.** more

Write the correct letter on the line at the end of each question.

1. What does the **er** affix mean in the word *longer*? __3__

2. What does the **er** affix mean in the word *zipper*? ____

3. What does the **er** affix mean in the word *talker*? ____

4. What does the **er** affix mean in the word *quicker*? ____

5. What does the **er** affix mean in the word *runner*? ____

6. What does the **er** affix mean in the word *clipper*? ____

Work with the teacher.

Match each word in Column A with its definition in Column B. Write the letter of your answer on the line.

Column A	Column B
_j_ 1. rocker	a. a person who jokes
____ 2. thinner	b. a thing that drains
____ 3. cutter	c. more wild
____ 4. cuter	d. a person who buys
____ 5. littler	e. more cute
____ 6. buyer	f. a person who dines
____ 7. wilder	g. more thin
____ 8. joker	h. a thing that cuts
____ 9. drainer	i. more little
____ 10. diner	j. a thing that rocks

Read this paragraph with the class or teacher.

THE HOME RUN KING

Babe Ruth was a gifted baseball player. He began playing baseball in 1914 as a left-handed pitcher. He was also noted as a home run hitter. In 1927, he hit 60 home runs in 154 games. Babe Ruth was elected to the Baseball Hall of Fame in 1936.

In the paragraph above, underline three words that contain the affix er, meaning *a person who*.

Read with the teacher.

Add er ("more") to a word when comparing two persons, places, or things that are different.

Example: Dan is strong. Kirk is stronger than Dan.

Use the word *than* with er when comparing two persons, places, or things.

Add the affix er to the word in parentheses to fill in the first blank. Use the word *than* in the second blank.

1. (short) I am __shorter__ __than__ the man in the black sport jacket.

2. (blue) Your eyes are _____ _____ mine.

3. (old) Verna is _____ _____ I am.

4. (fast) A horse can run _____ _____ a pony.

5. (quick) Traveling by plane is _____ _____ by train.

6. (tall) My wife is _____ _____ her sister.

7. (cold) The wind is _____ today _____ it was yesterday.

8. (hard) The last math test was _____ _____ the first one.

9. (large) Whales are _____ _____ dolphins.

10. (hot) It is _____ in the kitchen _____ it is in the hallway.

11. (thin) These pancakes are _____ _____ the ones I made last Sunday.

12. (small) Vermont and Kentucky are both _____ _____ Kansas.

13. (wide) The Hudson River is _____ _____ the Red River.

14. (pink) The sky was _____ at sunrise _____ it was at sunset.

Complete these sentences.

1. The forecast says that the weather will be _____ today

_____ it was yesterday.

2. The garage is closer to the house _____

_____.

3. _____ than a cat.

THE AFFIX EST

Work with the teacher.

The affix **est** is added to the end of a word to make it mean *the most*.

Example: tall + est = tallest (the most tall)

Join each root word and its affix.

1. large + est = _____largest_____ (the most large)

2. old   + est = _____ (the most old)

3. sad   + est = _____ (the most sad)

4. fine   + est = _____ (the most fine)

5. strict + est = _____ (the most strict)

Write the root word and its affix.

1. _____wet_____ + _____est_____ = wettest

2. _____ + _____ = kindest

3. _____ + _____ = bravest

4. _____ + _____ = thinnest

5. _____ + _____ = richest

6. _____ + _____ = straightest

Read these sentences with the class or teacher.

1. This is the mildest winter we've had since 1990.

2. The ostrich is the largest and strongest of living birds.

3. Which is the fastest way home?

4. Where is the safest place to swim?

5. Of all the states, Wyoming and Colorado have the straightest borders.

USING THE WITH THE AFFIX THAT MEANS THE MOST

Work with the teacher.

Add **est** to a word when comparing three or more persons, places, or things.

Example: Alex is the *strongest* of all those men.

Use *the* before a word with the affix **est** when comparing three or more persons, places, or things.

In the first blank, write the word *the*. In the second blank, add **est** to the word that is underlined.

1. It was <u>warm</u> on Tuesday. Wednesday was warmer than Tuesday. Thursday was _____ *the* _____ _____ *warmest* _____ day of all.

2. Atlanta is a <u>large</u> city. Denver is larger than Atlanta. Of the three, Boston is _____ _____.

3. This rose is <u>red</u>. That rose is redder than this one. Those roses by the fence are _____ _____ in the garden.

4. The Orange River is <u>long</u>. The Congo River is longer than the Orange. The Nile River is _____ _____ river in the world.

5. My car is <u>old</u>. Your car is older than mine. His car is _____ _____ in the parking lot.

6. Jinx is a <u>fat</u> cat. Tabby is fatter than Jinx. Tubby is _____ _____ in the litter.

7. The white sofa is <u>soft</u>. The black sofa is softer than the white sofa. The blue- and gold-striped sofa is _____ _____ in the store.

8. Brand X is <u>strong</u> coffee. Brand Y coffee is stronger than Brand X. Brand Z is _____ _____ coffee I've ever tasted.

9. The plane from Nashville will arrive <u>late</u>. The plane from Jackson will arrive later than the one from Nashville. The plane from Little Rock will arrive _____ _____ of all.

Complete these sentences.

1. The planet Mercury is _____ _____ planet to the sun.

2. The forecaster says that today is _____ day of the month.

3. You are _____ person I've ever met.

ANTONYMS

Work with the teacher.

Match each word in Column A with a word that means the *opposite* in Column B. Write the letter of your answer on the line.

Column A

_____ 1. hotter

_____ 2. thinnest

_____ 3. harder

_____ 4. larger

_____ 5. fastest

_____ 6. longest

_____ 7. taller

_____ 8. spender

_____ 9. tamest

_____ 10. louder

Column B

a. smallest

b. shorter

c. fattest

d. slowest

e. saver

f. colder

g. shortest

h. quieter

i. softer

j. wildest

FOLLOWING DIRECTIONS

Work with the teacher.

In row 1, put a check in front of the longest word.

In row 2, put a check in front of any word that is longer than the first word.

In row 3, put an **x** in front of the shortest word.

In row 4, put an **x** in front of any word that is shorter than the last word.

1. person	perch	perhaps	perky
2. skirt	squirm	stir	birth
3. curbs	curl	curve	church
4. bumper	blender	batter	blinker

Work with the teacher.

First, pronounce all of these words after the teacher. The teacher will then pronounce one word in each row. Listen, then circle that word.

1. waiter   water   wetter

2. sinner   singer   signer

3. tipper   taper   tapper

4. faster   fester   foster

5. rider   redder   raider

6. teller   taller   tiller

7. biker   baker   backer

8. seller   sadder   sitter

Join each word and its affixes.

1. stretch   +   er   +   s   =   _____

2. paint   +   er   +   s   =   _____

3. skate   +   er   +   s   =   _____

4. snip   +   er   +   s   =   _____

5. snipe   +   er   +   s   =   _____

6. log   +   er   +   s   =   _____

7. pitch   +   er   +   s   =   _____

8. win   +   er   +   s   =   _____

9. bake   +   er   +   s   =   _____

10. drum   +   er   +   s   =   _____

DICTIONARY PRONUNCIATION

Read the words in the box. On the blank next to each phonetic spelling, write the correct word from the list.

humble	husband	human	honest	humid
hunter	hundred	hurler	hurry	hummer

1. _____ hyōō mən

2. _____ hŭz bənd

3. _____ ŏn ĭst

4. _____ hŭm ər

5. _____ hůr e

6. _____ hyōō mĭd

DIVIDE AND MARK

In each of these names, the first syllable is the *strong* syllable. Divide each name and mark the vowels. Then add the accent mark.

1. Jason   _____Jā´ sən_____

2. Wilma   _____Wĭl mə_____

3. Joseph   _____

4. Cindy   _____

5. Ellen   _____

6. Adam   _____

WORD DICTATION

The teacher will dictate ten two-syllable words. Write the missing syllable. Then write the whole word.

First Syllable	*Second Syllable*	*Word*
1. tip	1. _____	1. _____
2. kill	2. _____	2. _____
3. pho	3. _____	3. _____
4. brave	4. _____	4. _____
5. mot	5. _____	5. _____
6. make	6. _____	6. _____
7. bat	7. _____	7. _____
8. hit	8. _____	8. _____
9. la	9. _____	9. _____
10. cop	10. _____	10. _____

Work with the teacher.

The details in a sentence—*Where? When? How?*—do not always follow the order of the headings in the grid. Sometimes words can be moved around in a sentence.

Examples: I met an old classmate at the mall (where) yesterday (when).

I met an old classmate yesterday (when) at the mall (where).

The same words are used in both sentences, but some of the words have been moved. In the second sentence, the words that tell *where* and *when* have changed places.

Examples: The commuter ate his lunch at the bus stop (where) in a hurry (how).

The commuter ate his lunch in a hurry (how) at the bus stop (where).

Once again, the same words are used in both sentences, but some of the words have been moved.

Read each sentence out loud. Put two lines under the subject and one line under the verb. Insert the sentences into the grid on the next page. Move the words around to make them fit the grid. Ask yourself each question at the top of the grid.

1. <u>People</u> <u>watched</u> the skydivers with amazement last Saturday.

2. The <u>movie</u> <u>starts</u> at 10 P.M. on TV.

3. A cricket chirped from time to time in the closet.

4. The driver will wait at the curb for a while.

5. Voters will go to the polls on Tuesday.

6. The hermit had lived by himself for a long time.

7. Mr. Baker began his trip with a full tank of gas yesterday.

8. The tall nurse puts her purse on the top shelf every day.

9. My landlord may travel by bike to Tampa in October.

10. The twins dressed alike most of the time.

Which? Whose? How Many?	SUBJECT Who? or What?	VERB Does? Did? Will Do?	OBJECT What? or Whom?	Where?	When? How Often? How Long?	How? Why?
1.	People	watched	the skydivers		last Saturday	with amazement
2.	The movie	starts		on TV	at 10 P.M.	
3.						
4.						
5.						
6.						
7.						
8.						
9.						
10.						

WORDS

_____   _____
_____   _____
_____   _____
_____   _____
_____   _____
_____   _____
_____   _____
_____   _____
_____   _____

WORD GROUPS

_____
_____
_____
_____
_____
_____

SENTENCES

_____
_____
_____
_____
_____
_____

The Scribal **o**

Read with the teacher.

A man named Gutenberg invented a printing press more than 500 years ago in Germany. Before that time, books were copied by hand. Such books were copied in monasteries by monks who were called *scribes. Scribe* means *a writer.*

Many of the scribes were Norman French, who did not fully understand the English language. They became confused when they tried to write or copy a language that they did not know well.

Sometimes the scribes would use the French letter **o** for the English short sound of the letter **u**. This happened especially when the **o** was next to the letters **m, n,** and **v**. As a result, we have words like *son, month,* and *love.*

The letter **o** that is pronounced /ŭ/ is sometimes called *the scribal* o.

Pronounce these words with the class or teacher. Then copy the words in the blanks below the box.

son	dove	front
ton	glove	monk
won	shove	month
none	above	sponge

_____   _____

_____   _____

_____   _____

_____   _____

_____   _____

_____   _____

Work with the teacher.

Pronounce these words with the class or teacher.

among	cover	covet	govern
hover	monkey	nothing	oven

Below are definitions of these words. The answers are given in the second column, but the vowels are missing. Fill in each blank with the correct word. Then write the word on the line.

Definition	Word	Write the Word
1. Not anything	n<u>o</u>th<u>i</u>ng	_____nothing_____
2. In the middle of	____m____ng	_____
3. To rule	g____v____rn	_____
4. To want something that belongs to someone else	c____v____t	_____
5. To stay close by; to stay in one place in the sky	h____v____r	_____
6. An enclosed space for baking	____v____n	_____
7. A small animal, related to the ape	m____nk____	_____
8. To place something on or over; to hide; to protect	c____v____r	_____

Divide these words into syllables. The **o** in the first syllable of each word is a scribal o. Place a small letter **u** over each scribal o. (The scribal o is always in a closed syllable.)

1. mother   _____mŏth_____ _____er_____

2. wonder   _____ _____

3. shovel   _____ _____

4. Monday   _____ _____

5. smother   _____ _____

6. honey   _____ _____

7. London   _____ _____

8. above   _____ _____

HOMOPHONES

Work with the teacher.

These words are homophones. Discuss the meanings with the teacher.

son	sun	won	one

Use the word in parentheses to help you complete each sentence.

1. (son) The father loved his _____.

2. (won) The hardest-working athlete _____.

You studied scribal o words in Student Books l and 2. These words were introduced as sight words.

of	from	come	some	one	done	love	money	tongue

Read this paragraph with the class or teacher. Then answer the questions below.

THE BIRD THAT HUMS

The *hummingbird* is the smallest of all birds. Its wings flutter so fast that they produce a hum. This tiny bird can hover over blossoms and other plants. While it hovers, it extracts insects, spiders, and nectar from the plants with its long tongue.

1. Which six words in the paragraph contain the scribal o?

_____

2. Why is this bird called a hummingbird? _____

3. In this paragraph, what does the word *nectar* mean?

_____

Work with the teacher.

The scribal o also appears in these common words. Pronounce them with the class or teacher.

color	dozen	other	another	brother

Fill in each blank with a word from the list above.

1. What _____ are you going to paint the kitchen?

2. Eight men ate two _____ Danish rolls.

3. My mother and her _____ went to a family gathering last month.

4. One gate was open and the _____ was shut.

5. The thirsty worker asked for _____ glass of water.

once

Read these sentences with the class or teacher.

1. We once lived in Fargo, North Dakota.

2. Once he starts talking, he never stops!

3. All at once, a huge cat lunged at us.

4. I like to be alone once in a while.

5. Sing that song once again.

6. Once upon a time, a handsome prince was turned into an ugly frog with warts.

Work with the teacher.

Read the sentences below. Each sentence contains an incorrect word. Cross out that word and write the correct word on the line.

1. A shopping center is one mile form my home. _____

2. Don't worry, we have plenty off time. _____

3. The usher asked the people in line not to shovel one another. _____

4. If you're cold, put another covet on the bed. _____

5. My brother one the race. _____

6. A park ranger told the campers to mother the campfire before they left. _____

The teacher will dictate 12 words.

1. _____   7. _____

2. _____   8. _____

3. _____   9. _____

4. _____   10. _____

5. _____   11. _____

6. _____   12. _____

PROVERB

Read this proverb with the class or teacher. Discuss its meaning.

Some of us are wise, and some are otherwise.

Work with the teacher.

Circle the word that does not belong with the group.

1. daisy   poppy   mother   pansy   lily

2. luster   above   gloss   sparkle   glitter

3. lark   gull   bluejay   brother   dove

4. blimp   among   glider   rocket   plane

5. front   fox   monkey   lizard   porcupine

6. scarlet   crimson   son   ruby   red

On the lines below, write all the words that you have circled.

1. _____   4. _____

2. _____   5. _____

3. _____   6. _____

Now put the words you have just written under the correct heading below.

Who?   **Where?**

_____   _____

_____   _____

_____   _____

Work with the teacher.

Write compound words.

1. some   + one   = _____

2. other   + wise   = _____

3. one   + self   = _____

4. over   + come   = _____

5. grand   + mother   = _____

6. none   + the + less   = _____

7. over   + done   = _____

8. mother + land   = _____

FOLLOWING DIRECTIONS

In row 1 and row 2, cross out any word that does not contain a scribal **o**. The first row has been done for you.

In row 3, underline the one word that contains a scribal **o**.

In row 4, put a check after any word that contains the *long* sound of **o**.

In row 5, put a check after any word that contains the *short* sound of **o**.

1. other   none   no

2. love   honey   hope

3. tone   done   note

4. oven   over   cover

5. drop   hot   son

PHONICS REVIEW

Work with the teacher.

First pronounce all of the words after the teacher. The teacher will then pronounce one word in each row. Circle that word.

1. win   wine   wane   won

2. dune   done   din   dine

3. bar   bare   buyer   burr

4. sign   son   sane   sin

5. bend   bond   boned   banned

6. ton   tone   tune   tan

7. came   cam   cone   come

8. bother   brother   butter   bather

Join each word and its affix or affixes.

1. govern   +   ment   = _____

2. com   +   ing   = _____

3. challenge +   er   = _____

4. sponge   +   y   = _____

5. a   +   shame   +   ed   = _____

6. trap   +   er   +   s   = _____

7. shove   +   ing   = _____

8. scratch   +   y   = _____

9. dozen   +   s   = _____

10. pave   +   ment   = _____

Work with the teacher.

DICTIONARY PRONUNCIATION

Read the words in the box. On the blank line next to each phonetic spelling, write the correct word from the list.

son	sponge	shovel	someone	smuggler
someday	spoke	shopper	smoker	smother

1. _____ smŭth ər

2. _____ sŭm wən

3. _____ spŭnj

4. _____ sŭn

5. _____ spōk

6. _____ shŭv əl

DIVIDE AND MARK

Each of these words has a schwa sound in one of the syllables. Divide each word and mark the vowels. Then add the accent mark. Remember, a syllable with a schwa is never the *strong* syllable.

1. model   _____ mŏd´ əl _____

2. hundred   _____ hŭn´ drəd _____

3. atop   _____

4. linen   _____

5. amass   _____

6. rodent   _____

WORD DICTATION

The teacher will dictate ten two-syllable words. Write the missing syllable. Then write the whole word.

First Syllable	*Second Syllable*	*Word*
1. _____	**1.** __nite__	**1.** _____
2. _____	**2.** __tane__	**2.** _____
3. _____	**3.** __tile__	**3.** _____
4. _____	**4.** __pose__	**4.** _____
5. _____	**5.** __lete__	**5.** _____
6. __tex__	**6.** _____	**6.** _____
7. __en__	**7.** _____	**7.** _____
8. __cos__	**8.** _____	**8.** _____
9. __u__	**9.** _____	**9.** _____
10. __im__	**10.** _____	**10.** _____

Work with the teacher.

Study these sentences:

1. A student parked her car at the edge of the campus.

2. At the edge of the campus, a student parked her car.

Both sentences say the same thing. The subject *student* tells who and the verb *parked* tells the action. The object *car* completes the action.

In the first sentence, the words that tell *where* come after the main part of the sentence. No comma is needed.

In the second sentence, the words that tell *where* have been moved to the beginning of the sentence. A comma is helpful here. *The comma lets us know that the main part of the sentence is coming.*

The purpose of a comma is to make a sentence easier to understand.

Read each sentence below out loud. Put two lines under the subject and one line under the verb.

Each sentence contains a group of words that tells where. Circle those words. The words that tell where come after the main part of the sentence, so no comma is needed.

Rewrite the sentences. Move the words that tell *where* to the beginning of the sentence. Use a comma after those words.

1. The <u>artist</u> <u>painted</u> a mural (on the other wall.)

   On the other wall, the artist painted a mural.

2. People formed a long line at the front box office.

   _____

3. A pie was baking in the oven.

   _____

4. The airplane hovered above some cliffs.

   _____

Details that tell *when* or *how* may also be moved to the beginning of a sentence. Use a comma to set them off.

Read each sentence below out loud. Put two lines under the subject and one line under the verb.

Each sentence contains a group of words that tells *when* or *how*. Circle those words.

1. Seven PTA <u>members</u> <u>met</u> (on the first Monday of October.)

   <u>On the first Monday of October, seven PTA members met.</u>

2. The coffee shop closed at 9 P.M.

   _____

3. A welder protects his eyes with safety glasses.

   _____

4. Ms. Miller buys a U.S. Savings Bond once a month.

   _____

5. That bricklayer installed the fireplace in just two days.

   _____

6. My sons were having a battle with wet sponges.

   _____

7. The tired man went to bed after dinner.

   _____

8. The bride phoned her brother before the wedding.

   _____

WORDS

_____ _____
_____ _____
_____ _____
_____ _____
_____ _____
_____ _____
_____ _____
_____ _____
_____ _____

WORD GROUPS

_____
_____
_____
_____
_____
_____

SENTENCES

_____
_____
_____
_____
_____
_____

Review

Work with the teacher.

Make new words by adding the ending affix **er** or **est** to each of these root words. Sometimes you can make only one new word. Other times you can make two.

Root	New Word	New Word
1. flat	flatter	flattest
2. surf	surfer	
3. thin		
4. sing		
5. strict		
6. fresh		
7. play		
8. firm		

In the word *driver,* write the part that means *a person who.*

_____

In the word *straighter*, write the part that means *more.*

_____

In the word *drainer,* write the part that means *a thing that.*

_____

The words below are all *sight words*, except for two. Cross these two words out. Then write the sight words in alphabetical order.

| says straight train again answer very clerk |

_____

_____

_____

_____

_____

Work with the teacher.

Each word in Column A contains an affix. First underline the affix. Then write the meaning of that affix next to it in Column B.

-ed	past tense of a verb	-ment	the act of
-ing	"doing" form of a verb	-er	a person
-s	s-form of a verb	-er	a thing that
-s	plural (more than one)	-er	more
-y	having or full of	-est	the most

Column A	**Column B**
1. curl<u>er</u>	a thing that
2. adults	_____
3. thirsty	_____
4. adopted	_____
5. lover	_____
6. government	_____
7. firmest	_____
8. squirms	_____
9. alerting	_____
10. stricter	_____

The verb in a sentence tells what the subject *did*. The object completes the action. It comes after the verb. Underline the object in each of these sentences.

1. The barber put his razor on the tray.

Circle the two words in the list below that begin with a schwa **a.**

after   agent   alley   afraid   alert

Work with the teacher.

Choose the correct word and write it in the blank.

1. Texas is _____ (smaller smallest) than Alaska.

2. The Grand Canyon is the _____ (larger largest) gorge in the world.

3. An SST jet can fly _____ (faster fastest) than a 707.

SPELLING THE SOUND /ÛR/

You have learned four ways to spell /ûr/.

Key Word	Spelling
clerk	**er** in a *strong* (stressed) syllable
girl	**ir**
nurse	**ur**
work	**or** after the letter **w**

Read this paragraph with the class or teacher.

The black skimmer is a water bird. It is black on top with a white tail and chest. It has a bill like a flat shovel. This bird works for its dinner in a strange way. It skims the top of the water, dragging the water for fish with the shovel-like bill.

In the paragraph above, circle the three one-syllable words that contain the /ûr/ sound (one word appears twice).

Change this question into a statement.

Has the actress fainted again?

1. _____

Now change the sentence into a negative statement by adding the word *not*.

2. _____

PART THREE

Lesson 11

Irregular Spelling Patterns—**ight**, **igh**, **ought**, **ould**

IGHT as in NIGHT

Read with the teacher.

The sounds of our language have changed. Eight hundred years ago, **gh** was pronounced with a rasping sound in the throat. Over the years, the **gh** combination went through some changes in pronunciation. Today, **gh** usually is not pronounced. In the words below, **gh** is silent.

Pronounce these words with the class or teacher.

light	flight	slight	sight	tight
right	bright	fright	fight	might

MAVERICK: Study this sight word with the teacher.

write

HOMOPHONES

These words are homophones. Discuss the meanings with the teacher.

right	write

Complete the sentence below using these two homophones.

My brother writes with his left hand, but I _____ with my

_____ hand.

IRREGULAR SPELLING PATTERNS—IGHT

Work with the teacher.

Choose a word from the list to match each definition. Write the word on the line.

bright	fight	flight	fright	light	might
night	right	sight	slight	tight	

1. _____light_____ not dark; bright; to set on fire; not heavy

2. _____ the time from sunset to sunrise

3. _____ the act of seeing; setting your eyes on something

4. _____ to struggle against; to quarrel; a battle or conflict

5. _____ the act of flying; steps (stairway)

6. _____ sudden alarm; shock; panic; fear

7. _____ sparkling; smart or clever

8. _____ opposite of left; correct

9. _____ not important; slim; slender

10. _____ firmly held together; very close; stretched

The word *lightning* was spelled lightening hundreds of years ago. Later the letter **e** was dropped.

Read these sentences with the class or teacher.

1. Lightning flashed across the dark sky.

2. Does lightning ever strike twice in the same place?

3. It lightninged just as I left home.

COMPOUND WORDS with IGHT

Work with the teacher.

Make compound words.

1. flash   +   light   =   _____

2. to   +   night   =   _____

3. eye   +   sight   =   _____

4. water   +   tight   =   _____

5. tail   +   light   =   _____

Divide these words into syllables.

1. lightning   _____   _____

2. twilight   _____   _____

3. tightwad   _____   _____

4. candlelight   _____   _____   _____

5. sightseeing   _____   _____   _____

6. oversight   _____   _____   _____

Read this paragraph with the class or teacher.

FIRST FLIGHT

Some people have always longed to fly. Over the ages, men and women have watched birds in flight. They have wondered, "Why can't we fly like birds?" At last, two brothers were named *Wright* (pronounced /rīt/). The Wright brothers made the first flight in 1903. That first flight lasted 12 seconds.

Use the dictionary to answer these questions.

1. What were the first names of the Wright brothers?

_____ and _____

2. Which brother was older? _____

3. Which brother lived longer? _____

IGH as in HIGH

Work with the teacher.

Pronounce these words with the class or teacher.

high	sigh	thigh

Choose a word from the box that matches a definition below. Write the word on the line.

1. The upper part of the leg _____

2. Tall; far above; important _____

3. To take a deep breath and let it out with a low sound

_____

Read these word groups with the class or teacher.

a sign on the highway

with a sigh

hurt his thigh

in the upper right-hand corner

a vast, bright band of light

Complete each sentence with one of the word groups above. Add a capital letter or period, if necessary.

1. The Milky Way is <u>a vast, bright band of light</u> that stretches across the sky.

2. Write your name _____ of the paper.

3. _____ said, NO LEFT TURN.

4. The star player _____ during the soccer game.

5. "Let's get to work," the tired boss said _____.

Use the dictionary to answer these questions.

1. Who was Florence Nightingale? _____

2. When was she born? _____

3. When did she die? _____

OUGHT

Read with the teacher.

The word *ought* means *should*. The word *to* and a base verb always comes after *ought*.

Examples: You *ought to take* an umbrella.

                 He *ought to pass* the test.

Read these sentences with the class or teacher. Put a circle around the word group that contains *ought* with the word *to* and the base verb form.

1. People ought to help fight the war on drugs.

2. He ought to come home.

3. You ought to see a dentist.

4. The party ought to be a lot of fun.

5. That shirt ought to fit you.

6. They ought to find jobs at the cannery.

7. She ought to enter the contest.

Read these words with the class or teacher. They contain the same *ought* spelling patterns.

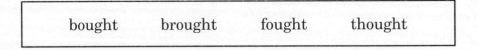

bought	brought	fought	thought

These words are used as the *past tense* of the words we will look at next.

Work with the teacher.

Study the following words. Notice that the affix **ed** is not added to the end of the words *buy, bring, fight,* and *think*. These are irregular verbs.

Base Form	Past Tense
buy	bought (*not* buyed)
bring	brought (*not* bringed)
fight	fought (*not* fighted)
think	thought (*not* thinked)

Copy each sentence. Change the underlined base form of the verb to the past tense.

1. From time to time, men <u>fight</u> in wars.

   <u>From time to time, men fought in the wars.</u>

2. Mark and Jack <u>buy</u> parts from Wholesale Car Supply.

   _____

3. People <u>think</u> the fire was started by lightning.

   _____

4. Armed guards <u>bring</u> cash to the bank.

   _____

5. They <u>buy</u> sandwiches and coffee for lunch.

   _____

6. My dog and cat <u>fight</u> in the backyard.

   _____

FOLLOWING DIRECTIONS

Work with the teacher.

The word *several* means *three or more, but not many.*

Several of these words contain an *ought* spelling pattern. Find and underline them. The first one has been done for you.

tight	<u>fought</u>	could	fight	sight	bright
would	slight	brought	mighty	ought	high
should	thigh	right	flight	sigh	thought

ANTONYMS

Draw a line from each word in the left column to a word that means the *opposite* in the right column.

bought   left

light   sold

bright   removed

right   dark

brought   dull

The teacher will dictate eight words and eight word groups.

Words	Word Groups
1. _____	9. _____
2. _____	10. _____
3. _____	11. _____
4. _____	12. _____
5. _____	13. _____
6. _____	14. _____
7. _____	15. _____
8. _____	16. _____

OULD

Read with the teacher.

Pronounce these words with the class or teacher.

would	could	should

Learn the spelling pattern of these three words as an **ould** unit. Only the beginning letters change.

Would, could, and *should* are helping verbs.

Would expresses a willingness to do something.

He would drive you home if you asked him.

Would helps to express a wish for something.

I would like apple pie for dessert.

Would indicates a habit of doing something regularly.

She would swim ten laps every day.

Would and could may be used to make polite requests.

Would you do that for me?
Could you do that for me?

Could can mean "able to."

Could you pick the children up at six?
(Will you be able to pick the children up?)

Most often should is used to mean *ought to*.

He should help his father fix the car.

Should also is used to express something that probably will happen.

They should arrive on Tuesday.

CONTRACTIONS WITH WOULD, COULD, AND SHOULD

Work with the teacher.

Write a contraction using *would* for each combination. The first word stays the same. The second word loses all letters except **d**.

1. I would   _____ I'd _____

2. he would   _____

3. she would   _____

4. you would   _____

5. we would   _____

6. they would   _____

Write the correct contraction in each blank.

1. _____ go with you if _____ drive me home later.
     (I would)   (you would)

2. The baby sitter said _____ be here by six.
                             (she would)

3. _____ like to buy tickets for the Red Sox game.
   (They would)

Write a contraction using *would*, *could*, and *should* for each combination.

1. would have   would've

2. could have

3. should have

WHAT'S MISSING?

Work with the teacher.

Read these sentences with the class or teachers. Something is wrong or missing. Make the corrections.

1. She couldve had the job, but she didn't want to drive so far.

2. That man shouldve helped the old lady up the steps.

3. We wouldve watched TV if we hadnt gone to a movie.

WRITE NEGATIVE CONTRACTIONS USING WOULD, COULD, AND SHOULD

1. would not   wouldn't

2. could not

3. should not

Read this paragraph with the class or teacher.

THE RED PLANET

You wouldn't want to travel to Mars. For one thing, it wouldn't be a quick trip. It would take you six months to get there. Once there, you couldn't get a drink of water or take a bath. Most of Mars is like a very cold desert. Intense dust storms often occur. These storms circle the entire planet and may last for months. The dust in the sky over Mars gives the planet a reddish color. It isn't likely that you'd be able to survive on the Red Planet.

In the paragraph above, underline the five words that are contractions.

Write contractions using *would, could,* and *should* for each combination.

1. he would   _____

2. would not   _____

3. could have   _____

4. should not   _____

5. you would   _____

6. could not   _____

7. they would   _____

8. would have   _____

Work with the teacher.

Circle the word that the teacher says.

1. mat   mate   might   mitt

2. but   bought   bait   bite

3. light   lit   let   late

4. wade   wide   wad   would

5. brat   bright   brute   brought

6. fact   fate   fight   fit

7. cud   could   code   cod

8. shad   shed   should   shod

Join each root word and its affix.

1. write   +   ing   = _____

2. sigh   +   ed   = _____

3. spot   +   ed   = _____

4. brave   +   est   = _____

5. snap   +   y   = _____

6. high   +   er   = _____

7. hire   +   ed   = _____

8. tape   +   ing   = _____

9. tap   +   ing   = _____

10. wet   +   est   = _____

Work with the teacher.

DICTIONARY PRONUNCIATION

Read the words in the list. On the blank next to each phonetic spelling, write the correct word from the list.

writer	thighs	first	straight	fighter
thirst	lightest	fright	sight	lightens

1. _____ lī´ tĕst

2. _____ fûrst

3. _____ rī´ tər

4. _____ strāt

5. _____ thīz

6. _____ frīt

DIVIDE AND MARK

These words contain a letter **y**, which is used as a vowel. Divide each word and mark the vowels long or short. Remember, when **y** is used as a vowel, it has the sound of /ē/, /ī/, or /ǐ/.

1. hobby   _____ häb′ē _____

2. typist   _____ tī′pǐst _____

3. standby   _____

4. candy   _____

5. skyline   _____

6. mystic   _____

WORD DICTATION

The teacher will dictate ten two-syllable words. Write the missing syllables. Then write the whole word.

First Syllable	*Second Syllable*	*Word*
1. bal	**1.** _____	**1.** _____
2. gos	**2.** _____	**2.** _____
3. meth	**3.** _____	**3.** _____
4. pen	**4.** _____	**4.** _____
5. rap	**5.** _____	**5.** _____
6. _____	**6.** lem	**6.** _____
7. _____	**7.** let	**7.** _____
8. _____	**8.** yon	**8.** _____
9. _____	**9.** tal	**9.** _____
10. _____	**10.** lon	**10.** _____

Work with the teacher.

You have learned that some sentences begin with a group of words that tell *where, when,* or *how.* We call this group an *introductory word group.* It introduces the rest of the sentence. *Use a comma after an introductory word group.* The comma "sets off" the introductory word group. That comma tells us that the main part of the sentence is coming. Remember that the main part of the sentence contains the subject and the verb and sometimes an object.

the main part of the sentence

Example: Every fall, the farmer harvests his crops.
                   (subject) (verb)   (object).

The words *Every fall* tell *when.* They come at the beginning, so they have a comma after them.

Each of the sentences below starts with a group of words that tells *where,* *when,* or *how.* The comma is missing. Read each sentence out loud. Put two lines under the subject and one line under the verb. Add a comma after the introductory word group.

1. On a high cliff, the <u>bird</u> <u>has laid</u> its eggs.

2. With a light blue crayon, an <u>artist</u> <u>was sketching</u> a face.

3. On Saturday night people swarmed to the playoff game.

4. Across the sky lightning flashed.

5. With a sigh the student began his homework.

6. In strong sunlight colors may fade.

7. Most of the time Gene writes with his right hand.

8. In 1903 the Wright brothers made their first flight.

9. With her birthday money the child bought a doll.

10. During the game a soccer player hurt his thigh.

Insert the sentences into the grid on the next page. Move the words around to make them fit the grid. Ask yourself each question at the top of the grid.

Which? Whose? How Many?	SUBJECT	VERB	OBJECT			
	Who? or What?	Does? Did? Will Do?	What? or Whom?	Where?	When? How Often? How Long?	How? Why?
1.	The bird	has laid	its eggs	on a high cliff		
2.	An artist	was sketching	a face			with a light blue crayon
3.						
4.						
5.						
6.						
7.						
8.						
9.						
10.						

WORDS

_____ _____

_____ _____

_____ _____

_____ _____

_____ _____

_____ _____

_____ _____

_____ _____

_____

WORD GROUPS

_____

_____

_____

_____

_____

SENTENCES

_____

_____

_____

_____

_____

The Affixes **less**, **ful**, and **ly**

THE AFFIX LESS

Work with the teacher.

The affix **less** is added to the end of a root word to make it mean without.

Examples: hope + less = hopeless (without hope)
               spot   + less = spotless (without a spot)

The affix **less** begins with a consonant. The silent e rule and the doubling rule do not apply.

Join each root word and its affix.

1. pain   + less = _____

2. rest   + less = _____

3. help   + less = _____

4. job   + less = _____

5. home   + less = _____

6. use   + less = _____

7. thank   + less = _____

8. sight   + less = _____

9. thought + less = _____

10. shape   + less = _____

Read with the teacher.

Use words from this box to complete the sentences below.

helpless	homeless	hopeless	jobless	painless
restless	sightless	thankless	useless	

1. Penguins cannot fly. They are _____flightless_____ birds.

2. The infant could not help herself. She was a _____ baby.

3. That cat has no home. It is _____.

4. The paper mill closed and those workers have no jobs. They are _____.

5. His cement mixer is broken and cannot be used. It is _____.

6. We cannot hope to find your contact lens in the parking lot. That is a _____ task.

7. I was not thanked for doing that job. It was a _____ job.

8. Some people find it hard to sit still for a long time. They get _____.

9. My dentist is very gentle and does not hurt me. I had a _____ visit to the dentist.

10. Fish that live in the dark waters of caves have no eyes. They are _____.

Work with the teacher.

The affix **ful** is added to the end of a word to make it mean *full of.* There is only one **l** in this affix.

Examples: hope + ful = hopeful (full of hope)
                pain + ful = painful (full of pain)

The affix **ful** begins with a consonant. The silent e rule and the doubling rule do not apply.

Join each root word and its affix.

1. wonder + ful = _____

2. use + ful = _____

3. thought + ful = _____

4. fright + ful = _____

5. hate + ful = _____

6. force + ful = _____

7. bliss + ful = _____

8. harm + ful = _____

The affix ful also means *full* or *as much as something can hold.*

Example: cup + ful = full (as much as a cup can hold)

Read these sentences with the class or teacher.

1. A trucker is getting a tankful of gas.

2. Mr. Mom drove a carful of kids to the park.

3. The carpenter grabbed a handful of nails.

4. You should add one more cupful of sugar to the cake batter.

5. That father and his sons bought a basketful of paper plates at the market.

THE AFFIX LY

Work with the teacher.

The affix **ly** is added to the end of a word to tell how something is done or *when* (how often) something happens.

Examples: sad   + ly = sadly
                 safe   + ly = safely
                 month + ly = monthly

"I lost my job," Carla said sadly.

How did she say it? *Sadly*

Peter arrived safely.

How did he arrive? *Safely*

The bills are due monthly.

When (how often) are the bills due? *Monthly*

The affix **ly** begins with a consonant. The silent e rule and the doubling rule do not apply.

Join each root word and its affix.

1. lone   +   ly   =   _____

2. night   +   ly   =   _____

3. glad   +   ly   =   _____

4. brave   +   ly   =   _____

Read these sentences with the class or teacher. Answer the questions that follow.

1. The inside of the church was dimly lighted. *How* was the church

   lighted? _____

2. That man takes a nightly walk with his two dogs. *When* (how often)

   does he take his dogs for a walk? _____

3. Mr. Hayworth quickly lined up his first grade students for a fire drill.

   How did Mr. Hayworth line up his students? _____

FOLLOWING DIRECTIONS

Work with the teacher.

The word *fewer* means "a smaller number of."

In row 1, row 2, and row 3, put a check in front of any word that has fewer letters than the first word in that row. The first one has been done for you.

In row 4, put a check after any word that has the same number of letters as the first word.

In row 5, put a check after any word that has the same number of letters, or more letters, than the first word.

1. helpful   helping   ✓helper

2. quickest   quicker   quickly

3. restless   rested   restful

4. thankful   thankless   thanking

5. smartly   smarter   smartest

The **ly** affix is often added to a root word as the *second* affix. The words below contain the affixes **less** and **ful** with **ly** added at the end.

Join each root word and its affixes. The first one has been done.

1. help   + less + ly = _____ *helplessly* _____

2. hope   + ful + ly = _____

3. rest   + less + ly = _____

4. use   + ful + ly = _____

5. thought   + ful + ly = _____

Write each root word and its affixes. The first one has been done for you.

1. <u>wonder</u>   +   <u>ful</u>   +   <u>ly</u>   =   wonderfully

2. _____   +   _____   +   _____   =   shamelessly

3. _____   +   _____   +   _____   =   painlessly

4. _____   +   _____   +   _____   =   playfully

5. _____   +   _____   +   _____   =   thoughtlessly

Read with the teacher.

Add the affix **ly** to the word in parentheses to make the word mean how something is or how something is done.

1. (restless) The athlete was waiting <u>restlessly</u> for his turn in the track event.

2. (thoughtful) He _____ bought his stepmother a dozen red roses for her birthday.

3. (painless) The nurse gave me the shot _____.

4. (rightful) That money is _____ mine.

5. (lifeless) The snake lay there _____.

6. (hopeful) He is waiting _____ for an answer.

7. (formless) The ghost _____ flitted into the dark graveyard at midnight.

8. (successful) My sister _____ completed her training in data processing.

9. (hopeless) That test was _____ hard!

10. (blissful) The tired mother relaxed in the warm bath water and

   sighed _____.

Complete these two sentences.

1. (thoughtless) My brother _____.

2. (Suddenly) The driver _____.

PHONICS REVIEW

Work with the teacher.

Circle the word that the teacher says.

1. fire   far   fir   four

2. fires   firs   farce   force

3. sod   sad   said   side

4. bran   brain   brine   bring

5. spire   spar   spur   spore

6. fuss   fuzz   fuse   phase

7. quit   quick   quack   quake

8. most   mist   messed   mast

Join each word and its affix or affixes.

1. hope + ing   = _____

2. hop + ing   = _____

3. hope + ful   = _____

4. hope + less   = _____

5. hop + ed   = _____

6. hope + ed   = _____

7. hope + s   = _____

8. hop + s   = _____

9. hop + er   = _____

10. hope + ful + ly = _____

Work with the teacher.

DICTIONARY PRONUNCIATION

Read the words in the box. On the blank next to each phonetic spelling, write the correct word from the list.

even	ever	endless	excess	exact
excite	enter	exam	extra	equal

1. _____ ĕg zăm´

2. _____ ĕk´ strə

3. _____ ĕv ər

4. _____ ē´ vən

5. _____ ĕg zăkt´

6. _____ ē´ kwəl

DIVIDE AND MARK

Each of these words contains a schwa sound in the second syllable. Divide each word and mark the vowels. Then add the accent mark. Remember not to separate the letters of a consonant digraph, such as **th** or **sh.**

1. ketchup   kĕtch′ əp

2. pocket   pŏck′ ĭt

3. chicken   _____

4. hatchet   _____

5. wholesome   _____

6. method   _____

WORD DICTATION

The teacher will dictate ten two-syllable words. Write the missing syllables. Then write the whole word.

First Syllable	*Second Syllable*	*Word*
1. du	1. _____	1. _____
2. mam	2. _____	2. _____
3. pub	3. _____	3. _____
4. ru	4. _____	4. _____
5. u	5. _____	5. _____
6. _____	6. gan	6. _____
7. _____	7. tal	7. _____
8. _____	8. let	8. _____
9. _____	9. mon	9. _____
10. _____	10. nus	10. _____

Work with the teacher.

In this lesson you learned that a word ending with the affix **ly** often tells how something is done.

Example: On the Fourth of July, bands marched briskly in the parade.

Each of the sentences below contains a word that tells how. Read each sentence out loud. Put two lines under the subject and one line under the verb. Some sentences contain an introductory word or word group and some do not. Add a comma if necessary.

1. Both ships sank rapidly.

2. Silently, the graceful dancer stepped onto the stage.

3. At the wedding a singer sang love songs softly.

4. Every evening traffic moves swiftly along Riverside Drive.

5. The father is tucking his son snugly into bed.

6. Lights are shining dimly in the tunnel.

7. Quickly Ben plunged his burned finger into ice water.

8. The spacecraft landed safely in the desert yesterday.

9. During the night stars glimmered brightly in the sky.

10. Restlessly a player is waiting on the sidelines.

Insert the sentences into the grid on the next page. Move the words around to make them fit the grid. Ask yourself each question at the top of the grid.

	SUBJECT	VERB	OBJECT			
Which? Whose? How Many?	*Who? or What?*	*Does? Did? Will Do?*	*What? or Whom?*	*Where?*	*When? How Often? How Long?*	*How? Why?*
1. Both	ships	sank				rapidly
2. The graceful	dancer	stepped		onto the stage		silently
3.						
4.						
5.						
6.						
7.						
8.						
9.						
10.						

WORDS

_____   _____
_____   _____
_____   _____
_____   _____
_____   _____
_____   _____
_____   _____
_____   _____
_____   _____
_____   _____

WORD GROUPS

_____
_____
_____
_____
_____

SENTENCES

_____

_____

_____

_____

_____

The Affixes less, ful, and ly

The Consonant **y** Spelling Rule

Work with the teacher.

RULE

If a word ends with **y,** look at the letter immediately before the **y**. If that letter is a *consonant* change the **y** to **i** when you add an ending affix.

Examples: h u r r (consonant) y + ed = hurr**i**ed
m e r c (consonant) y + ful = merc**i**ful
h a p p (consonant) y + ly = happ**i**ly

Join each word and its affix. First, circle the consonant immediately before the **y**. That will tell you to change the **y** to **i**. Then pronounce the words with the class or teacher. The first two have been done for you.

1. hap(p)y + ly = _____ happily _____

2. pi(t)y + ful = _____ pitiful _____

3. study + ed = _____

4. fancy + est = _____

5. mercy + ful = _____

6. nasty + ly = _____

7. cry + ed = _____

8. plenty + ful = _____

9. silly + er = _____

10. empty + ed = _____

11. ugly + est = _____

12. try + ed = _____

13. lazy + er = _____

14. dry + est = _____

15. sturdy + ly = _____

16. phony + est = _____

17. duty + ful = _____

18. body + ly = _____

19. cozy + est = _____

20. copy + ed = _____

Read these words with the class or teacher.

cozily	happily	merciful
studied	dried	flier
hurried	bodily	laziest
pitiful	phoniest	emptied
fancier	copied	silliest
denied	plentiful	uglier

Work with the teacher.

MAVERICKS: Study these sight words with the teacher.

any	**many**	**only**

Use a sight word from the box to complete each sentence.

1. _____ people would like to have that job.

2. _____ one person was hired for the job.

3. Are there _____ job openings at your workplace?

Fill in each blank. Use the root word and the affix given in parentheses.

1. (hurry + ed) When the concert was over, many people
_____ away.

2. (happy + ly) On payday, Mr. Purdy _____ stuffed his
paycheck into his pocket.

3. (copy + ed) Those graphs on the table will be _____ by
Myra and her staff.

4. (study + ed) Peter hardly ever _____ after a long day
at work.

5. (lazy + er) My dog is _____ than most dogs.

6. (angry + ly) "Don't print that!" a woman _____ told
the reporter.

7. (deny + ed) Only one child _____ that he ate the
candy.

8. (dry + est) This is the _____ summer that we have
ever had.

9. (nasty + ly) "Quit pushing!" the man snarled _____.

Work with the teacher.

If you are writing about more than one person, place or thing, or if you are using the **s form** of a verb, change the **y** to **i** and add **es**.

Examples: family + s = famil**ies**
                 try   + s = tr**ies**

Join each word and its affix. Pronounce the words with the class or teacher. The first one has been done for you.

1. story + s =   *stories*

2. party + s = _____

3. cry + s = _____

4. army + s = _____

5. empty + s = _____

6. jury + s = _____

7. body + s = _____

8. pity + s = _____

9. deny + s = _____

10. apply + s = _____

Pronounce these words, then answer the questions below.

parties	studies	pities
flies	tries	pennies
ladies	worries	copies

1. Which word rhymes with hurries? _____

2. Which two words rhyme with skies? _____ and _____

3. Which word has the sound of /a/ as in babies? _____

4. Which word rhymes with cities? _____

Work with the teacher.

Read this paragraph with the class or teacher.

A LANDLORD STORY

My landlord used to give backyard fly parties. He says that all of the flies on the block would come to those parties. Armies of flies would drop by for a snack. Even the tiniest fly was fond of hot dogs and French fries.

In the paragraph above, put a check in front of the six words that ended in **y** *before* the affix was added. Circle the one word that kept **y** when the affix was added.

FOLLOWING DIRECTIONS

In row 1, put an **x** after any word that has fewer letters than the last word in the row.

In row 2, put an **x** after any word that has more letters than the last word in the row.

In row 3, put a check after any word that has the same number of letters as the last word in the row.

In row 4, put a check after any word that has the same number of letters, or fewer letters, than the last word in the row.

1. story   replies   any   driest

2. empty   cries   pitiful   fried

3. many   lonely   spied   babies

4. armies   only   smoky   copier

PROVERB

Read this proverb with the class or teacher. Discuss its meaning.

Many hands make light work.

Work with the teacher.

The **y** does not change to **i** when an affix begins with **i**.

Examples: cry   + ing   =   crying (not criing)
                   hurry + ing   =   hurrying (not hurriing)

Join each word and its affix. Pronounce the words with the class or teacher.

1. study   + ing   = _____

2. worry   + ing   = _____

3. fly   + ing   = _____

4. empty   + ing   = _____

5. apply   + ing   = _____

6. spy   + ing   = _____

Read these word groups with the class or teacher.

are emptying   will be applying   is studying   were frying

Complete each sentence with one of the word groups above.

1. The hungry girls _____ bacon and eggs last night.

2. Two stock clerks _____ trash into the bins behind the store.

3. Lucas _____ for a driver license.

4. The tired student _____ past midnight.

Note: One word, *skiing,* has two i's together. The root word *ski* is a Norwegian word.

Work with the teacher.

Fill in each blank. Use the word and the affix given in parentheses.

1. (copy + ing) A clerk is _____ that memo for the files.

2. (rely + ing) You must stop _____ on others to do your work.

3. (deny + ing) Five campers are _____ that they started the forest fire.

4. (hurry + ing) The nurse was _____ to finish her report before the end of her shift.

5. (envy + ing) Victor won a sports car in the raffle, and everyone is

_____ him.

The teacher will dictate 20 words.

1. _____	6. _____	11. _____	16. _____
2. _____	7. _____	12. _____	17. _____
3. _____	8. _____	13. _____	18. _____
4. _____	9. _____	14. _____	19. _____
5. _____	10. _____	15. _____	20. _____

Work with the teacher.

If a word ends with a vowel + **y**, you keep the **y** when you add an affix.

Examples: Pla (vowel)y + ed = played (keep the **y**)
bu (vowel)y + ing = buying (keep the **y**)

Join each root word and its affix. Pronounce the words with the class or teacher.

1. stay + ed = _____

2. monkcy + s = _____

3. spray + er = _____

4. pray + ing = _____

5. turkey + s = _____

6. gray + est = _____

7. buy + er = _____

You have studied a few words that end in **ey**, such as *money, honey, monkey,* and *turkey.* Below is a more complete list of common English words that end in **ey**.

key	alley	attorney
jockey	valley	trolley
hockey	donkey	kidney

Work with the teacher.

Circle the word that does not belong with the group.

1. trolleys   monorails   always   subways   railways

2. donkey   turkey   lamprey   monkey   monthly

3. valley   hockey   soccer   polo   tennis

4. doctor   kidney   jockey   attorney   actor

5. kind   merciful   humane   forgiving   forever

6. muddy   dirty   alley   grimy   filthy

On the lines below, write all the words that you have circled.

1. _____   4. _____

2. _____   5. _____

3. _____   6. _____

Now put the words you have just written under the correct heading below.

What?   **When? How Often? How Long?**

_____   _____

_____   _____

_____   _____

Read with the teacher.

You have studied three words that do not follow the rule about keeping the **y** if a vowel comes before the **y**.

pay   paid   (not payed)

lay   laid   (not layed)

say   said   (not sayed)

Here are two more words that do not follow the rules.

day   daily   (not dayly)

slay   slain   (not slayed)

Use one of these words to complete each sentence below.

daily	laid	paid	said	slain

1. Dr. Thorp gently _____ the baby in the crib.

2. The mail arrives _____ at ten o'clock in the morning.

3. The pilot _____ that the flight would be slightly delayed.

4. The man was _____ by two murderers, who were sent to prison for life.

5. Have you _____ the water bill?

6. Jim _____, "I relied on you to finish that job."

7. To stay in shape, the women jog _____.

8. I _____ the paper on the table before I left. Where is it?

Work with the teacher.

Listen, then circle the word that the teacher says.

1. pure   purr   pore   par

2. lid   led   lad   laid

3. sign   sin   singe   sing

4. fist   fast   faced   phased

5. riffle   rifle   ruffle   raffle

6. taped   tapped   tipped   typed

7. slept   slapped   sloped   slopped

8. bats   batch   botch   badge

Join each word and its affix.

1. fun   +   y   = _____

2. funny   +   er   = _____

3. smoke   +   y   = _____

4. smoky   +   est   = _____

5. luck   +   y   = _____

6. lucky   +   ly   = _____

7. babe   +   y   = _____

8. baby   +   s   = _____

9. lone   +   ly   – _____

10. lonely   +   est   = _____

Work with the teacher.

DICTIONARY PRONUNCIATION

Read the words in the box. On the blank next to each phonetic spelling, write the correct word from the box.

plenty	pity	pretty	party	played
painless	playful	purple	people	partly

1. _____ pärt´ lē

2. _____ pān´ lĕs

3. _____ plā fəl

4. _____ prĭt´ ē

5. _____ plād´

6. _____ pē´ pəl

DIVIDE AND MARK

None of these words contains a schwa. Say each word out loud. Can you hear the strong syllable?

Divide each word and mark the vowels long or short. Then add the accent mark. (In three words, the second syllable is the strong syllable.)

1. motel   _mō tĕl´_

2. duplex   _dū´ plĕks_

3. fancy   _____

4. omit   _____

5. dentist   _____

6. hotel   _____

WORD DICTATION

The teacher will dictate ten two-syllable words. Write the missing syllables. Then write the whole word.

First Syllable	Second Syllable	Word
1. _____	1. ___ble___	1. _____
2. _____	2. ___zle___	2. _____
3. _____	3. ___tle___	3. _____
4. _____	4. ___dle___	4. _____
5. _____	5. ___tle___	5. _____
6. ___han___	6. _____	6. _____
7. ___lit___	7. _____	7. _____
8. ___sad___	8. _____	8. _____
9. ___dim___	9. _____	9. _____
10. ___puz___	10. _____	10. _____

Work with the teacher.

Each of these sentences contains a group of words that tells why.

Examples: The bus stopped to take on passengers. (why)
The worker was docked for being late.(why)

Read the first five sentences out loud. Put two lines under the subject and one line under the verb. Circle the words that tell why.

1. He bought two flannel shirts at the sale for his fishing trip.

2. A dozen men will work after dark with spotlights to finish the job.

3. A driver got a ticket for running a STOP sign.

4. The watchman drank coffee all night long to stay awake.

5. That waiter works hard for extra money.

The words *because of* are often used to introduce the reason why something happens.

Example: Four flights were delayed because of dense fog. (why)

Read the next five sentences out loud. Put two lines under the subject and one line under the verb. Circle the word groups that tell why.

6. The baby awoke because of a high fever.

7. My son called on Sunday because of my birthday.

8. Birds stayed away because of the cat.

9. Five men slept in a shelter last night because of the rain.

10. Those blankets have dried on the line quickly because of the hot wind.

Insert the sentences into the grid on the next page. Note that *Why?* has been added to the headings in the grid. Ask yourself each question at the top of the grid. The first two have been done for you.

	SUBJECT	VERB	OBJECT			
Which? *Whose?* *How Many?*	*Who? or What?*	*Does? Did? Will Do?*	*What? or Whom?*	*Where?*	*When?* *How Often?* *How Long?*	*How?* *Why?*
1.	He	bought	two flannel shirts	at the sale		for his fishing trip
2. A dozen	men	will work		after dark		with spot-lights to finish the job
3.						
4.						
5.						
6.						
7.						
8.						
9.						
10.						

WORDS

_____   _____
_____   _____
_____   _____
_____   _____
_____   _____
_____   _____
_____   _____
_____   _____
_____

WORD GROUPS

_____
_____
_____
_____
_____
_____

SENTENCES

_____
_____
_____
_____
_____
_____

The Vowel Combinations **ee** and **oa**

EE as in GREEN

Work with the teacher.

The **ee** combination is pronounced /ē/.

Pronounce these words with the class or teacher.

green	seem	freeze	deep	between
seen	feet	sneeze	sheep	indeed
teen	fleet	squeeze	sleep	succeed
heel	sheet	seed	asleep	exceed
wheel	street	speed	agree	needle
steel	teeth	sleeve	degree	steeple

Read these sentences with the class or teacher.

1. "Yes, indeed," said the salesman. "You'll get a free set of sheets if you buy this mattress."

2. Only thirteen workers at the steel mill went to the meeting last week.

3. The clock in the steeple isn't keeping correct time.

4. "Keep both hands on the wheel!" exclaimed the mother to her teenaged son.

5. Ms. Greeley got a ticket for exceeding the speed limit.

6. "Some day this seedling will be a tall evergreen tree," Kathleen told her grandson.

7. A fleet of ships could be seen in the distance.

8. "My feet hurt," mumbled the waiter. "These shoes are rubbing blisters on my heels!"

9. A sign in the park said, KEEP OFF THE GRASS.

10. That jeep is going the wrong way on a one-way street.

Work with the teacher.

Read this paragraph with the class or teacher.

A PEEP BECOMES A JEEP

In 1940, a small, all-purpose car was made for the U.S. Armed Forces. At first it was called a "peep." The peep was rugged like a truck, but it had the speed of a light car. It had four-wheel drive for deep mud and steep hills. The peep was also called "g.p." (short for *general-purpose* vehicle). Later, the letters "g.p." became the word *jeep*.

In the paragraph above, circle the eight words that contain the **ee** combination.

knee   kneel

Write the *pronunciation* of each of these words. Use the dictionary.

1. knee   _____

2. kneel   _____

Write these words in alphabetical order.

beet   _____

kneel   _____

jeep   _____

beetle   _____

greet   _____

beef   _____

Greece   _____

knee   _____

Work with the teacher.

Choose a word from the box that matches a definition below. Write the word on the line.

breeze	kneel	speech	week
cheek	queen	steel	weep
cheese	reek	steep	
knee	screech	sweet	

1. The way sugar or honey tastes _____

2. A strong metal _____

3. Seven days _____

4. To cry or sob _____

5. The leg joint between the thigh and shin _____

6. To give off a strong or bad smell _____

7. A gentle wind _____

8. A public talk or address; the act of talking _____

9. The side part of the face _____

10. This is made from milk. _____

11. A woman ruler _____

12. A shrill, harsh cry _____

13. Very high; having a high, sharp slope _____

14. To rest on one or both knees _____

Read with the teacher.

Some words with the **ee** combination are irregular verbs. The affix *ed* is not added to the end of these words in the past tense. This type of verb is very old and has been in the English language for hundreds of years.

Pronounce these words with the class or teacher.

Base Form	Past Tense	Base Form	Past Tense
keep	kept	meet	met
sleep	slept	feed	fed
weep	wept	bleed	bled
sweep	swept	speed	sped
feel	felt	flee	fled
kneel	knelt	breed	bred

Fill in each blank with the past tense of the verb in parentheses.

1. Mr. Keeler _____ his money safely in a bank.
   (keep)

2. A medic _____ the pulse of the injured man.
   (feel)

3. Huge waves _____ the raft onto shore.
   (sweep)

4. The child _____ when she stepped on a nail.
   (weep)

5. Wildlife _____ the raging forest fire.
   (flee)

6. Most of the passengers _____ during the flight.
   (sleep)

7. A cut on his finger __ _____ badly for a while.
   (bleed)

8. They _____ in the coffee shop at one o'clock.
   (meet)

9. The farmer _____ extra hay to the hungry horses.
   (feed)

10. Traffic _____ along the freeway.
    (speed)

11. She _____ to pull weeds in the garden.
    (kneel)

12. Those ranchers _____ cattle for beef.
    (breed)

MAVERICK: Study this sight word with the teacher.

been

Read these sentences with the class or teacher.

1. You have been late every day this week.

2. On his days off, the painter has been painting his front porch.

3. A dozen forest rangers have been working overtime this summer.

4. Mr. Keeler has been a cab driver for almost ten months.

Read the sentences below. Each sentence contains an incorrect word. Cross out that word and write the correct word on the line.

1. Have you ~~seem~~ my green shirt? _____*seen*_____

2. The baby has bin asleep all morning. _____

3. I will met them in the hotel lobby. _____

4. Do you fell sick? _____

5. We need tree copies of that contract. _____

6. Were have you been? _____

7. Those people seen to be lost. _____

PROVERBS

Read these proverbs with the class or teacher. Discuss the meaning of each one.

1. The grass is always greener on the other side of the fence.

2. Still waters run deep.

3. One tree doesn't make a forest.

Work with the teacher.

Divide these words into syllables.

1. feeble _____ _____   **4.** freedom _____ _____

2. canteen _____ _____   **5.** succeed _____ _____

3. agree _____ _____   **6.** needle _____ _____

THE COMBINATION EE AS AN R-CONTROLLED VOWEL

If the letter **r** comes after the **ee** combination, the sound of **ee** is similar to a short i (ĭ).

On the first line, write the pronunciation of each word. On the second line, write the meaning of the word. Use the dictionary.

	Pronunciation	*Meaning*
1. deer	_____	_____
2. cheer	_____	_____
3. peer	_____	_____
4. sneer	_____	_____
5. career	_____	_____

Two words with the **ee** combination are the same whether they mean *one* animal or *more than one: deer* and *sheep.* Do not add the affix **s** to these words.

Fill in each blank with the word in parentheses.

1. (deer) One _____ was running beside the freeway.

2. (deer) Three other _____ were running in the forest.

3. (sheep) The mother _____ lost her lamb.

4. (sheep) All of the _____ in the flock were grazing by the fence.

Work with the teacher.

Make words with the ee vowel combination by using consonants. The first one has been done for you.

Write Eight Words

_____ reef _____

_____

_____

_____

_____

_____

_____

_____

The teacher will dictate eight words and eight word groups.

Words

1. _____

2. _____

3. _____

4. _____

5. _____

6. _____

7. _____

8. _____

Word Groups

9. _____

10. _____

11. _____

12. _____

13. _____

14. _____

15. _____

16. _____

Read with the teacher.

The vowel combination **oa** is pronounced /ō/. The letter **a** is silent. The **oa** combination is used at the beginning or in the middle of a word.

Pronounce these words with the class or teacher. Then copy the words in the blanks below the box.

boat	goal	loan	toast
coat	coal	moan	roast
road	soap	roar	oak
load	loaf	soar	soak

1. _____

2. _____

3. _____

4. _____

5. _____

6. _____

7. _____

8. _____

9. _____

10. _____

11. _____

12. _____

13. _____

14. _____

15. _____

16. _____

Match each word in Column A with its definition in Column B. Use the dictionary if you need to. Write the letter of your answer on the line.

Column A	Column B
1. ___ boar	**a.** A male pig; a wild pig with tusks
2. ___ boast	**b.** Tiny bubbles that form on liquid; froth
3. ___ cloak	**c.** To trick; a joke
4. ___ foal	**d.** A baby horse
5. ___ foam	**e.** To brag; to praise oneself
6. ___ hoax	**f.** A coat with no sleeves; to cover or hide

Read with the teacher.

Two words in the **oa** spelling need special attention.

1. board

The word *board* is pronounced with the long **o** sound. This word can be a problem because it so closely resembles this sight word: *broad*.

MAVERICK: Study this sight word with the teacher.

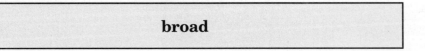

broad

The sight word, *broad*, begins with the consonant blend **br**, and the **oa** combination has the sound of /ô/, as in "dog."

Compare: board   broad

2. hoarse

The word *hoarse* means a *gruff or harsh sound in the throat.* It is pronounced with the long **o** sound (ō). This word looks and sounds similar to the word *horse* (pronounced /hôrs/).

Draw a line between word groups in Column A and Column B to form complete sentences.

Column A	Column B
1. A steel bridge	were hoarse from yelling.
2. Ms. Shoal has bought	spans the broad river.
3. Fans at the soccer game	skateboards on the sidewalk.
4. Kids can't ride	a small shop on Broadway.
5. Ponies are the smallest	to board the train.
6. Thirty people were waiting	of all horses.

Work with the teacher.

First pronounce the words in the box. Then choose a word that matches a definition below. Write the word on the line.

coach	coast	float	groan
oar	oath	roach	throat

1. The front part of the neck between the chin and the collarbone.

   _____

2. A sworn statement to tell the truth; a pledge _____

3. A person who trains athletes; a railroad car _____

4. To moan; a deep sound made in the throat _____

5. A paddle used to move and steer a boat _____

6. To move or drift in a free way; to be held up by water

   _____

7. Shoreline; to glide or drift along _____

8. An insect; a common pest that lives in damp places

   _____

HOMOPHONES

Discuss the meaning of these homophones with the teacher.

soar	road	sore	rode

Each of these sentences contains one of the above homophones. First underline each homophone. Then complete the sentences in your own words.

1. The airplane will soar _____ (where?)

2. His knee has been sore _____ (how long?)

3. A woman crossed the road _____ (when?)

4. The salesman rode from one end of town to the other

   _____ (how?)

DIVIDING WORDS THAT CONTAIN VOWEL COMBINATIONS

Read with the teacher.

A word that contains a vowel combination is usually divided after the second vowel.

Example: needle   nee/dle   (Divide after the second vowel.)

Sometimes, a word with a vowel combination is divided between consonants.

Example: seedling   seed ling   (Divide between consonants.)

Divide these words into syllables with a slash (/). *Remember: Do not divide between the two vowels in a vowel combination.*

1. frccdom
2. boatload
3. feeble
4. boastful

5. deeply
6. peevish
7. soapsuds
8. steeple

9. cheetah
10. coastline
11. coatless
12. beetle

Read these pairs of words with the class or teacher.

Compare

cot	coat	bat	boat
got	goat	hard	hoard
rod	road	horse	hoarse
clock	cloak	or	oar
cost	coast	of	oaf

FOLLOWING DIRECTIONS

Among the words below, you will find several sight words. Circle them.
(The word *among* means *somewhere in the group.*)

knee	sweep	bleed	feed	been
beef	kneel	asleep	boat	groan
oath	soak	broad	coast	float

The Vowel Combinations ee and oa

Work with the teacher.

Circle the word that the teacher says.

1. cut   cute   cot   coat   cat

2. feel   fell   fill   full   foal

3. flat   float   fleet   flit   flight

4. bait   bat   beet   bet   boat

5. click   clack   cloak   clock   cluck

6. slop   slope   slip   sleep   slept

7. got   goat   gut   get   gait

8. ride   rid   rod   road   rude

Join each word and its affix or affixes.

1. freeze + er = _____

2. coach + s = _____

3. daisy + s = _____

4. breeze + y = _____

5. pity + ful = _____

6. slop + y = _____

7. cheer + ful + ly = _____

8. broad + est = _____

9. tweeze + er + s = _____

10. groan + ed = _____

SYLLABLE PRONUNCIATION

Read the words in the box. On the blank next to each phonetic spelling, write the correct word from the box.

squeezes	screened	sleepy	sloppy	speedy
sleeves	squeegee	soaked	second	soapy

1. _____ sĕk´ ənd

2. _____ slē´ pē

3. _____ sōkt

4. _____ skwēz´ ēs

5. _____ sō´ pē

6. _____ skwē´ jē

DIVIDE AND MARK

Each of these place names contains a schwa sound. Divide each word and mark the vowels. Then add the accent mark.

1. Richmond   __Rĭch mənd__

2. Jackson   __Jăck sən__

3. Ogden   _____

4. Trenton   _____

5. Salem   _____

6. Denver   _____

WORD DICTATION

The teacher will dictate ten two-syllable words. Write the missing syllables. Then write the whole word.

First Syllable	_Second Syllable_	_Word_
1. ____ex____	1. _____	1. _____
2. ____col____	2. _____	2. _____
3. ____ad____	3. _____	3. _____
4. ____lil____	4. _____	4. _____
5. ____um____	5. _____	5. _____
6. _____	6. ____cy____	6. _____
7. _____	7. ____vade____	7. _____
8. _____	8. ____mute____	8. _____
9. _____	9. ____dred____	9. _____
10. _____	10. ____mune____	10. _____

Work with the teacher.

Each of these sentences contains an *introductory word group* that tells *why*. Read each sentence out loud. Add a comma after the introductory word group. (Remember that an introductory word group comes at the beginning of a sentence.) Put two lines under the subject and one line under the verb. The first two have been done for you.

1. To save the forest, <u>firefighters</u> <u>fought</u> the blaze for three days.

2. Because of a coal strike, the <u>miners</u> <u>are</u> <u>picketing</u>.

3. For his fine work Mr. Fleet got a bonus.

4. Because of a sore throat Janet stayed home yesterday.

5. To smother the ashes the campers put dirt by the handful on the dying fire.

6. Because of the fumble we lost the ball on the one-yard line.

Insert the sentences into the grid on the next page. Move the words around to make them fit the grid. Ask yourself each question at the top of the grid.

7.–8. Write two sentences of your own in the grid. The verbs have been given. Then copy your sentences on the lines below the grid.

Which? Whose? How Many?	SUBJECT Who? or What?	VERB Does? Did? Will Do?	OBJECT What? or Whom?	Where?	When? How Often? How Long?	How? Why?
1.	firefighters	fought	the blaze		for three days	to save the forest
2.	The miners	are picketing				because of a coal strike
3.						
4.						
5.						
6.						
7.		was sleeping				
8.		will load				

DICTATION

WORDS

_____	_____
_____	_____
_____	_____
_____	_____
_____	_____
_____	_____
_____	_____
_____	_____
_____	_____

WORD GROUPS

_____

_____

_____

_____

_____

SENTENCES

_____

_____

_____

_____

_____

_____

Review

Work with the teacher.

SPELLING THE LONG SOUND OF I

So far, you have learned five ways to spell /i/.

Key Word

Dime	**i** with a silent **e** at the end of a word.
Pilot	**i** at the end of an open syllable
Type	**y** with a silent **e** at the end of a word
My	**y** at the end of an open syllable
High	**igh**

Read this paragraph

The pack rat is a large rodent with a bushy tail. He has a quaint lifestyle. He likes to hoard. In the daytime, he hides. At night, he travels far and wide to collect things for his nest. He dresses up his home with shiny objects such as metal buttons and buckles. He even collects and saves thorny bits of cactus.

In the paragraph above, underline the seven words that contain the long sound of **i**.

Read these sentences. Put a comma after the introductory word group. Put two lines under the subject and one line under the verb. Remember, sometimes the verb is made up of two words.

1. On Main Street the lights are blinking.

2. Next Saturday our son will compete in a track meet.

Work with the teacher.

Make a new word by adding the ending affix **less, ful,** or **ly** to each of these root words.

Root	New Word	Root	New Word
1. stain	_____	**5.** penny	_____
2. part	_____	**6.** happy	_____
3. force	_____	**7.** pity	_____
4. week	_____	**8.** speech	_____

SPELLING THE LONG SOUND OF O

So far, you have learned three ways to spell /o/.

Key Word	Spelling
Vote	**o** with a silent **e** at the end of the word
Motel	**o** at the end of an open syllable
Boat	**oa**

Read this paragraph.

A jellyfish has no bones. It seems to float harmlessly, but nobody likes to be stung by it.

In the paragraph above, underline the four words that contain the long sound of o (ō).

Circle the word that tells *who* or *what* in each word group. Then underline the word that tells *which*, *whose*, or *how many*.

truthful (witness)   one girl   longest coastline
small feet   shirtless man   her brother

Work with the teacher.

ANTONYMS

Choose a word from the list that means the opposite of each word listed below. Write your answer on the line.

drier	emptied	happily	ladies	ugliest

1. sadly   _____

2. filled   _____

3. prettiest   _____

4. wetter   _____

5. gentlemen   _____

So far, you have learned four ways to spell /e/.

Key Word	Spelling
Eve	**e** with a silent **e** at the end of the word
Female	**e** at the end of an open syllable
Happy	**y** at the end of a two-syllable word
Green	**ee**

Read this paragraph.

    In some places, nomads roam the desert. They even bring the children with them. These nomads keep herds of sheep, goats, and cattle. They must move often to find grassy spots so the herds can feed.

In the paragraph above, underline the five words that contain the long sound of **e**.

Change this question into a statement.

    Was the traffic speeding on Broadway?

1. _____

    Now change the sentence into a *negative* statement by adding the word *not*.

2. _____

PART FOUR

Lesson 16

The Affixes **re** and **un**

THE AFFIX RE

Work with the teacher.

The affix **re** is added to the beginning of a word to make it mean *again* or *back*.

Examples: re + fill   =   refill (fill again)
                       re + pay   =   repay (pay back)

Join each root word and its affix or affixes.

1. re + call   = _____

2. re + pack   = _____

3. re + turn   = _____

4. re + set   = _____

5. re + train   = _____

6. re + order   = _____

7. re + act   + ing = _____

8. re + hire   + ed = _____

9. re + fresh + ing = _____

10. re + type + ed = _____

Work with the teacher.

There are three common words that change pronunciation when the affix **re** is added to them. The /s/ sound in *sign, serve,* and *side* changes to a /z/ sound.

re + sign (re zīn´)   Bob will *resign* from his job in October.
re + serve (re zûrv´)   I will *reserve* a ticket for you.
re + side (re zīd´)   They *reside* in a duplex in Denver.

Below is a box of words that contain the affix **re**. Write the correct word to complete each sentence.

recall	reserved	reside
resigned	retired	returned

1. Two families _____ (live) in that duplex.

2. Ms. Broadwell _____ (quit) her job as a sales clerk.

3. Do you _____ (remember) your license plate number?

4. The waiter _____ (came back) to the table with a menu.

5. You can pick up your _____ (saved for later use) tickets at the box office.

6. Dr. Reed is 65, and he is _____ (no longer doing his lifework).

Work with the teacher.

The affix **un** is added to the beginning of a word to make it mean *not*.

Examples: un + safe = unsafe (not safe)
un + able = unable (not able)

Join each root word and its affix or affixes.

1. un + happy = _____

2. un + kind = _____

3. un + even = _____

4. un + limited = _____

5. un + luck + y = _____

6. un + snap + ed = _____

7. un + like + ly = _____

8. un + settle + ing = _____

9. un + think + ing + ly = _____

10. un + re + move + ed = _____

Write the root word and its affixes.

1. _____ + _____ + _____ = unsightly

2. _____ + _____ + _____ = untruthful

3. _____ + _____ + _____ = unplanned

4. _____ + _____ + _____ = unused

Work with the teacher.

Read these sentences to the teacher.

1. Someone left the fried chicken uncovered, and a dozen flies are having a picnic.

2. The falcon gazed at us with unblinking eyes.

3. A girl ran for the bus with her jacket unzipped and her shoelaces untied.

4. The rewind button on this tape recorder is jammed.

5. Three government agents uncovered clues in a bank scandal.

6. An attorney asked the judge to reopen the murder case.

7. A woman was unjustly accused of the crime.

8. Unthinkingly, Sam didn't put money in the parking meter and got a ticket.

FOLLOWING DIRECTIONS

The word *between* means *in the space that separates two objects or things.* For example, in a toasted cheese sandwich, the cheese is between two slices of toast.

In row 1, row 2, and row 3, put a check after the word that is between two words beginning with the affix **re**. The first row has been done for you.

1. coach   retype   order✓   rehired

2. freezer   refill   reef   replay

3. resign   bloated   retrain   wheels

In row 4 and row 5, put an **x** after the word that is between two words beginning with the affix **un**.

4. unlikely   poach   untrue   weekly

5. untied   speech   unjust   unite

Work with the teacher.

Make a new word by adding the beginning affix **un** or **re** to each of these root words.

1. paid _____

2. made _____

3. charge _____

4. load _____

5. fund _____

6. well _____

7. sure _____

8. fresh _____

9. cover _____

10. afraid _____

11. stable _____

12. locate _____

1. In the word *repaint,* write the part that means *again.*

2. In the word *untold,* write the part that means *not.*

3. In the word *recall,* write the part that means *back.*

4. In the word *unwanted,* write the part that means *not.*

Read this paragraph with the class or teacher.

MY FICKLE BROTHER

My brother is the most fickle person I've ever met. Last Friday, he resigned his job, packed his bags, and left the city. On Monday, he reported to my mother by phone that he was getting tired of living alone. On Tuesday, he repacked his bags, reloaded the trunk of his car, and returned home. We watched him unload the trunk and unpack his bags. On Wednesday, my fickle brother went to his old boss and got rehired. He's fickle, but he's not unlucky!

Read the above paragraph again. Put an **x** in front of the six words that begin with the affix **re**. Underline the three words that begin with the affix *un*.

Discuss the meaning of the last sentence.

Work with the teacher.

Circle the word that the teacher says.

1. met   meet   mitt   might   mate

2. cast   cost   coast   cyst   kissed

3. soap   sop   sip   seep   sap

4. choke   chock   check   cheek   chick

5. waiter   water   wetter   wider   whiter

6. shun   shine   sheen   shin   shone

7. tossed   toast   taste   test   text

8. week   wick   walk   wake   whack

Join each word and its affix.

1. tire + ed = _____

2. try + ed = _____

3. shake + y = _____

4. agree + ment = _____

5. hurry + ed = _____

6. pray + ed = _____

7. copy + er = _____

8. mercy + ful = _____

9. sad + ly = _____

10. sad + est = _____

Work with the teacher.

DICTIONARY PRONUNCIATION

Read the words in the list. On the blank next to each phonetic spelling, write the correct word from the list. Notice that the affix **re** is an open syllable pronounced /rĭ/ in many words. In these words, the accent is on the root word.

recall	remark	reckless	reclaim	regain
remind	reddish	restless	riddle	request

1. _____ rĕk´ lĕs

2. _____ rĭ´ märk

3. _____ rĭ gān´

4. _____ rĭ kôl´

5. _____ rĭ kwĕst´

6. _____ rĭd´ əl

DIVIDE AND MARK

Each of these words contains a schwa sound. Divide each word and mark the vowels. Then add the accent mark. (Two words have the schwa in the first syllable.) The first two have been done for you.

1. closet   _clŏs´ĭt_

2. frozen   _frō´zən_

3. item   _____

4. alike   _____

5. robin   _____

6. connect   _____

WORD DICTATION

The teacher will dictate ten two-syllable words. Write the missing syllables. Then write the whole word.

First Syllable	*Second Syllable*	*Word*
1. graph	1. _____	1. _____
2. pam	2. _____	2. _____
3. dol	3. _____	3. _____
4. pho	4. _____	4. _____
5. si	5. _____	5. _____
6. _____	6. ph	6. _____
7. _____	7. phan	7. _____
8. _____	8. phid	8. _____
9. _____	9. seph	9. _____
10. _____	10. ics	10. _____

Work with the teacher.

Read each sentence out loud. Some contain an introductory word group and some do not. Add a comma if necessary. Put two lines under the subject and one line under the verb.

1. At this moment, <u>Ms. Hogan</u> <u>is retyping</u> the sloppy letter.

2. On the Red Planet, dust <u>storms</u> <u>occur</u> often.

3. The doctor reduced the swelling with an ice pack.

4. On Wednesday his old boss rehired my lucky brother.

5. To restart the printer I will press this switch.

6. Because of unsafe tires the truck skidded on the icy road.

7. The diner thanked the waitress for refilling the coffee mug.

8. After next September the Goldbergs will relocate on the West Coast.

9. A person may put soft drink cans in that container for recycling.

10. Some workers are removing the old sidewalk with a jackhammer.

Insert the sentences into the grid on the next page. Ask yourself each question at the top of the grid.

Which? Whose? How Many?	SUBJECT	VERB	OBJECT			
	Who? or What?	Does? Did? Will Do?	What? or Whom?	Where?	When? How Often? How Long?	How? Why?
1.	Ms. Hogan	is retyping	the sloppy letter		at this moment	
2. dust	storms	occur		on the Red Planet	often	
3.						
4.						
5.						
6.						
7.						
8.						
9.						
10.						

WORDS

_____   _____
_____   _____

_____   _____
_____   _____

_____   _____
_____   _____

_____   _____
_____   _____

WORD GROUPS

_____
_____
_____
_____
_____
_____

SENTENCES

_____
_____
_____
_____
_____
_____

The Vowel Combination **ou**

OU as in HOUSE

Read with the teacher.

By far the most common sound for the **ou** combination is a *gliding* sound. First you hear /ŏ/, then /oo/. One sound glides smoothly into the other.

Pronounce these words with the class or teacher.

house	round	out	our
mouse	around	scout	sour
blouse	ground	about	scour
loud	pound	count	flour
aloud	sound	county	devour
cloud	south	scout	ounce
proud	mouth	amount	bounce

HOMOPHONES

Discuss the meanings of these homophones with the teacher.

our   hour

Complete these sentences using the homophones *our* and *hour*.

1. The shuttle bus was on time, but _____*our*_____ plane left an

   _____*hour*_____ late.

2. It takes one _____ to drive from _____
   house to yours.

3. _____ son was born about an _____ after
   the doctor arrived.

4. The _____ hand on _____ alarm clock is
   stuck.

5. We waited around for an _____ in the rain before

   _____ bus came.

Work with the teacher.

Choose a word from the box that matches a definition below. Write the word on the line.

couch	foul	grouch	hound	pouch
scour	shout	snout	spouse	trout

1. To yell; a loud cry _____

2. Husband or wife; a mate _____

3. A hunting dog; to nag or pester _____

4. A sofa _____

5. A small bag or sack _____

6. A person who complains; to grumble or complain _____

7. The long nose of an animal _____

8. A kind of fish _____

9. To scrub or rub hard _____

10. Evil; dirty; in baseball, a ball batted outside the lines

_____

The Vowel Combination ou

doubt

Write the *pronunciation* of each of these words. Use the dictionary.

1. doubt   _____

2. mountain   _____

3. council   _____

Complete each sentence with *doubt, mountain,* or *council.*

1. Last night, a _____ meeting was held at City Hall.

2. I _____ that it will rain today.

3. The Cascade Range is a _____ chain in the Northwest.

Work with the teacher.

Make compound words.

1. with   +   out   =   _____

2. under   +   ground   =   _____

3. out   +   side   =   _____

4. south   +   west   =   _____

5. house   +   hold   =   _____

6. out   +   come   =   _____

7. round   +   about   =   _____

8. thunder   +   cloud   =   _____

Divide these words into syllables with a slash (/).

1. amount	5. around	9. countless
2. trousers	6. scoundrel	10. doubtful
3. announce	7. thousand	11. fountain
4. mouthful	8. surround	12. pronounce

ANTONYMS

Draw a line from each word in Column A to a word that means the opposite in Column B.

Column A	*Column B*
north	loud
sweet	out
soft	sour
lost	south
humble	found
in	proud

The Vowel Combination ou

Work with the teacher.

The words *mouse* and *louse* have irregular plurals.

One	More Than One
(Singular)	(Plural)
mouse	mice
louse	lice

Fill in each blank with one of the words above.

1. I spotted one _____ on my dog yesterday.

2. The vet said that my dog has _____ and will have to be "dipped."

3. "Dipping" gets rid of _____ on dogs and cats.

4. Five pesky _____ were running around the house.

5. One _____ scampered under the couch.

6. Four _____ devoured a small bag of crackers.

Write the PLURAL form of each word. Check your answers in a dictionary.

1. mouth _____   6. county   _____

2. spouse _____   7. louse   _____

3. mouse _____   8. thousand _____

4. couch _____   9. sheep   _____

5. deer _____   10. goose   _____

Read with the teacher.

Below are some common abbreviations for weight, time, and distance. Memorize them.

Weight

l lb.   =   pound (from the Latin word li<u>b</u>ra)

oz.   =   ounce or ounces (16 ounces   =   1 pound)

Time

hr.   =   hour (60 minutes)

min.   =   minute (60 seconds)

sec.   =   second

Distance

mi.   =   mile (5,280 feet or 1.609 kilometers)

Distance in time

mph   =   miles per hour

or m.p.h.

(This may be written with or without periods.)

Read these word groups to the teacher.

clocked at 82 mph by the highway patrol officer.

bought a 5 lb., 8 oz. watermelon

not more than 10 mi. from this spot

listening to the 2 ½ hr. broadcast

galloped ½ mi. in 1 min. and 13 sec.

FOLLOWING DIRECTIONS

Work with the teacher.

In each row, cross out any word that is between two words that start with the letter *s*.

1. shout   amount   south   sound   mouth

2. cloud   stout   sour   pouch   spouse

3. scour   ouch   snout   doubt   scout

Read this paragraph with the class or teacher.

UFOs

    UFOs are objects or lights in the sky that cannot be explained. Thousands of UFO sightings have been reported. UFO reports come from around the world. Some people are afraid that we will be invaded by strange beings from outer space. Experts doubt that we will be invaded, but they cannot account for some UFOs. Most UFOs are just bright planets, large birds, planes, huge kites, or falling stars.

In the paragraph above, circle the five words that contain the ou combination.

Use the dictionary to answer these questions.

1. What do the letters UFO stand for? _____

2. How many syllables are in *unidentified?* ____

Work with the teacher.

Circle the word that the teacher says.

1. mass   moss   mouse   muss   muse

2. full   foul   foal   fall   fell

3. sound   sand   send   sinned   signed

4. laid   led   lied   loud   load

5. his   he's   hose   whose   house

6. fund   fond   found   find   fanned

7. groaned   ground   grand   grind   grinned

8. bind   band   bend   bound   bond

Join each word and its affix or affixes.

1. wonder + ful   = _____

2. cloud + y   = _____

3. pouch + s   = _____

4. alley + s   = _____

5. worry + s   = _____

6. ground + less   = _____

7. doubt + ful   = _____

8. flat + est   = _____

9. dirt + y   + er = _____

10. re + count + ed = _____

Work with the teacher.

DICTIONARY PRONUNCIATION

Read the words in the box. On the blank next to each phonetic spelling, write the correct word from the list.

outer	otter	order	oath	over
other	often	ounce	oven	once

1. _____ ŭth´ ər

2. _____ ō´ vər

3. _____ ōth

4. _____ ŭv´ ən

5. _____ ȯf ən

6. _____ ouns

DIVIDE AND MARK

Some of these words contain a schwa sound, some do not. Divide each word and mark the vowels. Then add the accent mark. In one word, the second syllable is the *strong* syllable.

1. local   _____lō′ kəl_____

2. chisel   _____chĭz′ əl_____

3. holy   _____

4. contain   _____

5. frantic   _____

6. magnet   _____

WORD DICTATION

The teacher will dictate ten two-syllable words. Write the missing syllables. Then write the whole word.

First Syllable	*Second Syllable*	*Word*
1. cy	1.	1.
2. hy	2.	2.
3. gyp	3.	3.
4. ty	4.	4.
5. sym	5.	5.
6.	6. stic	6.
7.	7. tem	7.
8.	8. thon	8.
9.	9. press	9.
10.	10. lon	10.

Work with the teacher.

Words that tell *which, whose,* or *how many* often come in front of a word that tells *who* or *what.* You are familiar with the column heading *Which? Whose? How Many?* in the grid. This column comes before the subject (who or what).

In this lesson, you will be working with two or three words that tell something about the subject.

Example: Our two old cars are parked in the driveway.

        cars tells what (the subject)
        our tells whose cars
        two tells how many cars
        old tells which cars

Below is a list of word groups that contain a subject and two or three words that tell something about the subject. Circle the words in each group that tell *which*, *whose*, or *how many*. Put two lines under the subject. The first one has been done for you.

My (five) barking <u>hounds</u>   A dozen red blouses

That empty playground   Her loud TV

A large hilltop house   Those three lofty mountains

One grouchy customer   The oldest scout

Select one of the word groups above to complete each sentence. Then insert the sentences into the grid on the next page. Ask yourself each question at the top of the grid. The first one has been done for you.

1. <u>My five barking hounds</u> remained in the kennel for a week.

2. _____ woke the people in the next apartment.

3. _____ are hanging on the sale rack.

4. _____ rise above the clouds.

5. _____ helped the other scouts willingly.

6. _____ fills quickly during lunch hour.

7. _____ complained loudly.

8. _____ lost its porch because of a mudslide.

	SUBJECT	VERB	OBJECT			
Which? Whose? How Many?	*Who? or What?*	*Does? Did? Will Do?*	*What? or Whom?*	*Where?*	*When? How Often? How Long?*	*How? Why?*
1. My five barking	hounds	remained		in the kennel	for a week	
2.						
3.						
4.						
5.						
6.						
7.						
8.						

Vowel Combinations—More Sounds for **ou**

OU as in YOU

Read with the teacher.

Eight common words are spelled with the ou combination that sounds like /oo/.

Two words come from the old English language.

you   youth

Six words come from the French language.

soup   tour   route

group   detour   coupon

The words *route* and *coupon* each have two acceptable pronunciations. On the lines below, write the two pronunciations for each word. Use the dictionary.

1. route _____   _____

2. coupon _____   _____

Match each word in Column A with its definition in Column B. Write the letter of your answer on the line.

Column A	Column B
1. ____ coupon	a. Opposite of I or me
2. ____ detour	b. A sightseeing trip
3. ____ group	c. Not an adult; a young person
4. ____ route	d. A road, way, or path
5. ____ tour	e. A roundabout route that takes the place of the main route
6. ____ you	f. A printed ad or ticket that can be used to get a discount on items
7. ____ youth	g. A number of persons or things close together

Work with the teacher.

Read these word groups with the class or teacher.

on his mail route

a group of fans

did you tour

will have to take a detour

three cans of chicken soup

youths of today

Complete each sentence with one of the word groups above. Add a capital letter or period, if necessary.

1. Cut out this coupon and you'll save seventy cents on

_____.

2. _____ the White House when you were in Washington?

3. That stretch of road is being repaved, so you _____.

4. He walks five miles a day _____.

5. _____ from Houston shouted and cheered loudly at the playoff game.

6. _____ are taller and stronger than those of the past.

through

Write the word *through* in each blank to complete the sentence. Read the sentences with the class or teacher.

1. We drove _____ Bucks County on our way to Camden.

2. Corey found a job _____ the want ads in the paper.

3. A sign at the corner said, "Not a _____ Street."

4. Our dog escaped _____ a hole in the backyard fence.

OU as in FOUR

Work with the teacher.

The **ou** combination is pronounced /ô/ in a few English words.

four   pour   court   course

The word *course* has several meanings. Write three definitions for the word *course*. Use the dictionary.

1. _____

2. _____

3. _____

Using the words *four, pour, court,* and *course,* complete these sentences.

1. Twenty-six people are taking a _____ (what?) in welding.

2. _____ (How many?) drivers got tickets on that stretch of highway.

3. The judge called the _____ (what?) to order.

4. Two adults will _____ (do?) drinks for the children.

The teacher will dictate eight words and eight word groups.

Words	*Word Groups*
1. _____	9. _____
2. _____	10. _____
3. _____	11. _____
4. _____	12. _____
5. _____	13. _____
6. _____	14. _____
7. _____	15. _____
8. _____	16. _____

Read with the teacher.

Some words have an **ou** combination that is pronounced /ŭ/ (short **u**).

All of the following words come from the French, except *young*. The word *young* comes from the Old English language.

Pronounce these words with the class or teacher.

double	cousin	couple	touch
trouble	country	young	

Fill in the blanks with one of the words in the box.

1. If the photographer can get that job in Portland, he'll be able to

   _____ his income.

2. Mrs. Nelson and her _____ are so much alike that people think they are twins.

3. The alderman had car _____ on the freeway and was late for the city council meeting.

4. Mr. Moneybags spent his lottery winnings on a cross-

   _____ tour.

5. That elderly lady seems very _____ for her age.

6. The man warned, "Don't _____ that wire! You might get a shock!"

7. Will you lend me a _____ of quarters for the parking meter?

Work with the teacher.

The vowels are missing in one word in each sentence below. Fill in the missing vowels. Then write the whole word on the line.

1. Does your son have a paper r ____ ____ t ____? _____

2. I have to be in traffic c ____ ____ rt at l0 a.m. on Tuesday morning.

_____

3. Next summer we're moving to a house in the c ____ ____ n tr ____.

_____

4. My youngest brother finished a bartending c ____ ____ r s ____ last

month. _____

5. Mr. Panzer works at the c ____ ____ n t ____ courthouse.

_____

6. I bought some Blitz Bug Spray today. Those roaches in my kitchen are

in deep t r ____ ____ bl ____! _____

7. A huge truck that pulls two trailers is called a d____ ____ b l ____.

_____

Read this paragraph with the class or teacher.

A LANDLORD STORY

My landlord was born on a farm. The farmhouse was so small that he had to sleep in the barn when he was young. He slept in a stall with a horse, but he snored so loudly that the horse kicked him out.

Circle the one **ou** word in the paragraph above that has the sound of /ŭ/.

Work with the teacher.

Circle the word that does not belong with the group.

1. always	forever	never	proudly	endlessly
2. cloudy	daily	sunny	foggy	rainy
3. outside	tree	hedge	bush	grass
4. soup	sandwich	salad	pudding	coupon
5. marmot	mouse	chipmunk	trout	squirrel
6. quickly	swiftly	hourly	speedily	rapidly
7. country	county	highway	state	city
8. sickly	loudly	ill	unwell	ailing

On the lines below, write all the words that you have circled.

1. _____

2. _____

3. _____

4. _____

5. _____

6. _____

7. _____

8. _____

Now put the words you have just written under the correct heading below.

What?	*Where?*	*When?*	*How?*
_____	_____	_____	_____
_____	_____	_____	_____

Work with the teacher.

FOLLOWING DIRECTIONS

In row 1, underline any word that has more letters than the first word.

In row 2 and row 3, cross out any word that does not have more letters than the first word.

1. group   detour   soup   tour

2. course   four   court   pour

3. double   touch   young   country

Read these proverbs with the class or teacher. Discuss the meaning of each.

1. Every cloud has a silver lining.

2. It never rains but it pours.

Make words with the ou vowel combination by using consonants. Write ten words. The first one has been done for you.

hound

_____

_____

_____

_____

_____

_____

_____

_____

_____

Work with the teacher.

Circle the word that the teacher says.

1. bat   but   bout   boat   bought

2. soup   soap   sop   sip   seep

3. gripe   grip   grape   grope   group

4. prude   proud   prod   prayed   pride

5. rote   rot   rut   route   write

6. skit   scat   skate   Scot   scout

7. shout   shot   shut   shoat   sheet

8. less   lace   lass   loss   louse

Join each word and its affix.

1. ice   +   y   = _____

2. icy   +   er   = _____

3. deny   +   ed   = _____

4. country   +   s   = _____

5. county   +   s   = _____

6. slap   +   ed   = _____

7. course   +   s   = _____

8. fret   +   ed   = _____

9. bone   +   y   = _____

10. nasty   +   ly   = _____

Work with the teacher.

DICTIONARY PRONUNCIATION

Read the words in the box. On the blank next to each phonetic spelling, write the correct word from the list.

alone	album	abroad	able	about
abode	aboard	abound	alight	allot

1. _____ ə bōrd´

2. _____ ā´ bəl

3. _____ ə līt´

4. _____ ăl´ bəm

5. _____ ə bout´

6. _____ ə bōd´

DIVIDE AND MARK

Divide each word and mark the vowels. Then add the accent mark. In one word, the second syllable is the *strong* syllable.

1. system ____sĭs´ təm____

2. hobo ____hō´ bō____

3. plenty _____

4. comet _____

5. vital _____

6. commit _____

WORD DICTATION

The teacher will dictate ten two-syllable words. Write the missing syllables. Then write the whole word.

First Syllable	Second Syllable	Word
1. _____les_____	1. _____	1. _____
2. _____ex_____	2. _____	2. _____
3. _____un_____	3. _____	3. _____
4. _____com_____	4. _____	4. _____
5. _____hab_____	5. _____	5. _____
6. _____	6. _____net_____	6. _____
7. _____	7. _____lide_____	7. _____
8. _____	8. _____lid_____	8. _____
9. _____	9. _____ond_____	9. _____
10. _____	10. _____close_____	10. _____

Work with the teacher.

Read each sentence out loud. Add a comma if necessary. Put two lines under the subject and one line under the verb. Then insert the sentences into the grid on the next page.

1. My young <u>cousin</u> <u>found</u> a job through the want ads.

2. In a little while, the busy <u>waiter</u> <u>will serve</u> the soup.

3. To save money we use coupons.

4. Every spring the county spends our tax money to fix muddy roads.

5. Those bad roads delayed the tour bus for four hours.

6. Twenty tired tourists complained bitterly.

7.–8. Write two sentences of your own in the grid. (The verbs have been given.) Ask yourself each question at the top of the grid. Then copy your sentences on the lines below the grid.

Which? Whose? How Many?	SUBJECT	VERB	OBJECT			
	Who? or What?	Does? Did? Will Do?	What? or Whom?	Where?	When? How Often? How Long?	How? Why?
1. My	cousin	found	a job			through the want ads
2. The busy	waiter	will serve	the soup		in a little while	
3.						
4.						
5.						
6.						
7.		was shouting				
8.		poured				

WORDS

_____   _____

_____   _____

_____   _____

_____   _____

_____   _____

_____   _____

_____   _____

_____   _____

_____   _____

_____   _____

WORD GROUPS

_____

_____

_____

_____

_____

_____

_____

_____

_____

_____

SENTENCES

_____

_____

_____

_____

_____

_____

The Affixes **able** and **ness**

THE AFFIX ABLE

Work with the teacher.

The affix **able** is added to the end of the word to make it mean "able to be." When it is added to a root word, *able* is pronounced /ə bəl/.

Examples: like + able = likeable (able to be liked)
                 wash + able = washable (able to be washed)

Join each root word and its affix. Drop the silent e in the root word before adding *able*.

1. print + able = _____

2. stretch + able = _____

3. love + able = _____

4. use + able = _____

5. move + able = _____

6. train + able = _____

7. cure + able = _____

8. work + able = _____

9. quote + able = _____

10. port + able = _____

Work with the teacher.

Fill in each blank by adding *able* to the end of the root word that is in italics.

Example: His coat is dirty, but it can be *wash*ed.
It is _____washable_____.

1. The dishwasher was old, but it still could be *used*.
It was still _____.

2. Many breeds of dogs are *train*ed to help blind people.
Those dogs are _____.

3. Everyone *like*s the twins.
They are _____ children.

4. Your plan might *work*.
It seems like a _____ plan.

5. The papers *quote*d the comments of the councilman
His comments were _____.

6. She is very sick with an ulcer, but it can be *cured*.
That type of ulcer is _____.

7. We *understand* why you were so angry.
Your anger was _____.

8. The blue denim pants are tight, but they can be *stretch*ed.
They are _____.

THE AFFIX NESS

Work with the teacher.

The affix **ness** is added to the end of a word to make it mean "having the quality of."

Examples: dark + ness = darkness (having the quality of being dark)

   kind + ness = kindness (having the quality of being kind)

Join each root word and its affix.

1. thick   +   ness   =   _____

2. mild   +   ness   =   _____

3. swift   +   ness   =   _____

4. fresh   +   ness   =   _____

5. sad   +   ness   =   _____

6. happy   +   ness   =   _____

7. like   +   ness   =   _____

8. empty   +   ness   =   _____

The affix **ness** often is used with other affixes. It usually is the last affix used in a word.

Join each root word and its affixes.

1. thought   +   ful   +   ness   =   _____

2. rest   +   less   +   ness   =   _____

3. love   +   ly   +   ness   =   _____

4. sleep   +   y   +   ness   =   _____

5. use   +   ful   +   ness   =   _____

Work with the teacher.

Read these word groups with the class or teacher. Add a period at the end of each sentence.

in the thickness of the fog

his kindness to the children

in the stillness of the forest

the sadness in her eyes

Complete each sentence with one of the word groups above.

1. One sailboat was lost _____.

2. The woman seemed happy, but we could see _____.

3. A group of mothers thanked the young officer for

_____.

4. A deer feels safe _____.

MAVERICK: Study the sight word with the teacher.

> **business**

Write the *pronunciation* of the word *business*. _____

The root word of *business* is *busy*, which you studied in Student Book 2, Lesson 7. The **y** changes to **i** when the affix **ness** is added.

Read these sentences with the class or teacher.

1. My cousin runs a small business in Key West.

2. Those two partners have a business agreement.

3. A businesswoman called about the sale of our home.

4. That young teenager is businesslike in handling his paper route.

ANTONYMS

Work with the teacher.

An antonym is a word that means the *opposite* of another word.

Match each word in Column A with its antonym in Column B. Write the correct letter on the line to the left.

Column A

1. ____ hopefulness

2. ____ helplessness

3. ____ thanklessness

4. ____ usefulness

5. ____ thoughtlessness

Column B

a. uselessness

b. thoughtfulness

c. hopelessness

d. thankfulness

e. helpfulness

FOLLOWING DIRECTIONS

In row 1, underline any word that has fewer letters than the first word.

In row 2 and row 3, cross out any word that does not have fewer letters than the first word.

1. unprintable   kindness   sleeplessness   portable

2. business   usable   unworkable   sadness

3. youthfulness   thickness   understandable   lovable

Work with the teacher.

Circle the word that the teacher says.

1. all   ail   I'll   ill   eel

2. rise   raise   razz   rouse   rose

3. roll   rule   rail   reel   rile

4. chuck   chock   choke   cheek   chick

5. fight   fought   feet   fit   fat

6. bail   ball   bell   bill   bile

7. pale   pal   peel   pull   poll

8. bat   boat   but   bought   bet

Join each word and its affixes.

1. un   + hurry + ed = _____

2. settle + er   + s   = _____

3. love   + ing   + ly = _____

4. un   + luck + y   = _____

5. youth + ful   + ness = _____

6. farm   + er   + s   = _____

7. re   + type + ing = _____

8. un   + fold + ed = _____

9. craze + y   + ness = _____

10. re   + use   + able = _____

Work with the teacher.

DICTIONARY PRONUNCIATION

Read the words in the box. On the blank next to each phonetic spelling, write the correct word from the box.

illness	ice	item	immune	eyes
ignite	inches	injury	amuse	invite

1. _____ ĭn´ jər ē

2. _____ ĭz

3. _____ ə myooz´

4. _____ īs

5. _____ ĭg nīt´

6. _____ ī´ təm

DIVIDE AND MARK

Divide each word and mark the vowel. Then add the accent mark. In two words, the second syllable is the *strong* syllable.

1. hiccup   hĭk´ kŭp

2. tempo   tĕm´ pō

3. supply   _____

4. even   _____

5. confuse   _____

6. lobby   _____

WORD DICTATION

The teacher will dictate ten two-syllable words. Write the missing syllables. Then write the whole word.

First Syllable	Second Syllable	Word
1. vic	1. _____	1. _____
2. ex	2. _____	2. _____
3. hu	3. _____	3. _____
4. bap	4. _____	4. _____
5. cab	5. _____	5. _____
6. _____	6. tal	6. _____
7. _____	7. pel	7. _____
8. _____	8. bute	8. _____
9. _____	9. quest	9. _____
10. _____	10. mate	10. _____

Work with the teacher.

Read each sentence out loud. Add a comma if necessary. Put two lines under the subject and one line under the verb. Then insert the sentences into the grid on page 295. The first one has been done for you.

1. During the day <u>Mr. Grotsky</u> <u>runs</u> a pest control business.

2. Because of the darkness Mrs. Richmond tripped.

3. In the middle of the night our lovable infant wants a bottle.

4. The lost tourists thanked the officer for his helpfulness.

5. Every so often this useful beeper makes a sound.

6. Scott brought his portable stove to the campsite.

7.–8. Write two sentences of your own on the grid. (The verbs have been given.) Ask yourself each question at the top of the grid. Then copy your sentences on the lines below the grid.

Which? Whose? How Many?	SUBJECT	VERB	OBJECT				
	Who? or What?	Does? Did? Will Do?	What? or Whom?	Where?	When? How Often? How Long?	How? Why?
1.	Mr. Grotsky	runs	a pest control business		during the day	
2.						
3.						
4.						
5.						
6.						
7.		is writing				
8.		washed				

WORDS

_____   _____

_____   _____

_____   _____

_____   _____

_____   _____

_____   _____

_____   _____

_____   _____

_____   _____

WORD GROUPS

_____

_____

_____

_____

_____

_____

SENTENCES

_____

_____

_____

_____

_____

_____

The Affixes able and ness

Review

Read with the teacher.

Each word in Column A contains an affix. First, underline the affix. Then write the meaning of that affix on the line under Column B.

Here is a list of affix meanings:

s	plural (more than one)	**ful**	full or full of
y	having or full of	**ly**	tells "how"
er	a person who	**re**	again
er	more	**un**	not
est	the most	**able**	able to be
less	without	**ness**	having the quality of

Column A	Column B
1. countri<u>es</u>	<u>plural (more than one)</u>
2. regroup	_____
3. youthful	_____
4. loudest	_____
5. unbound	_____
6. cloudy	_____
7. shouter	_____
8. doubtless	_____
9. proudly	_____
10. touchable	_____
11. younger	_____
12. soundness	_____

Work with the teacher.

Write the word each abbreviation stands for. Choose from these words:
pound, ounce, hour, minute, second, mile, miles per hour.

1. min. _____ **4.** oz. _____ **6.** lb. _____

2. sec. _____ **5.** mi. _____ **7.** mph _____

3. hr. _____

Make a new word by adding the affix able or ness to each of these root words.

Root	New Word	Root	New Word
1. pay	_____	**7.** clever	_____
2. bright	_____	**8.** forgive	_____
3. tax	_____	**9.** explain	_____
4. loud	_____	**10.** bitter	_____
5. adapt	_____	**11.** happy	_____
6. sick	_____	**12.** transport	_____

Find the sight word and underline it.

loud   outside   couch   doubt   mouth   shout

Write the root word and its affixes.

1. _____ + _____ + _____ = skillfully

2. _____ + _____ + _____ = soundlessness

3. _____ + _____ + _____ = unzipped

4. _____ + _____ + _____ = reusable

5. _____ + _____ + _____ + _____ = undoubtedly

Work with the teacher.

Read the sentences below. Each sentence contains an incorrect word.
Cross out that word and write the correct word on the line. Each of the
correct words has an **ou** combination.

1. The United States is our county. _____

2. We grabbed a quick lunch—grilled cheese sandwiches, chicken soap,
   and coffee. _____

3. My wife is in charge of our horsehold. _____

4. The mother told her teenaged son to take his feet off the coach.
   _____

ANTONYMS

Write an antonym for each of the underlined words below. The words in
your answers must all contain **ou** as in *house*.

1. <u>Yours</u> is the opposite of _____*ours*_____.

2. <u>Lost</u> is the opposite of _____.

3. <u>North</u> is the opposite of _____.

4. <u>Sweet</u> is the opposite of _____.

5. <u>Quiet</u> is the opposite of _____.

Read these sentences. Put a comma after the introductory word group.
Circle the subject and underline the verb. Remember, the verb is
sometimes made up of two words.

1. Until an hour ago the copier was working.

2. In the Southwest the sun is shining brightly.

Change this question into a statement.

Is that couch sagging in the middle?

1. _____

Now change the sentence into a negative statement by adding *not*.

2. _____

A. Write the contraction for each combination. (11 points)

1. it is   _____

2. I am   _____

3. will not   _____

4. you will   _____

5. are not   _____

6. cannot   _____

7. we have   _____

8. do not   _____

9. they are   _____

10. Madam   _____

11. of the clock _____

B. Match each word in Column A with its definition in Column B. Write the letter of your answer on the line next to the number. (7 points)

Column A	*Column B*
____ **1.** aid	**a.** market
____ **2.** carve	**b.** map; graph
____ **3.** chart	**c.** to move from side to side
____ **4.** forgive	**d.** to cut up
____ **5.** trail	**e.** help
____ **6.** mart	**f.** path
____ **7.** sway	**g.** to excuse; to pardon

C. Divide these words into syllables with a slash (/). (4 points)

1. complain _____   3. absorb _____

2. maintain _____   4. always _____

D. Write the abbreviation for each day of the week. (7 points)

1. Sunday _____

2. Friday _____

3. Tuesday _____

4. Wednesday _____

5. Saturday _____

6. Thursday _____

7. Monday _____

E. Draw a line from each word in the left column to its definition in the right column. (4 points)

tail   a story

tale   the end of something; the back part

sale   the selling of something at a reduced price

sail   to move across water in a ship or craft

F. Join each word and its ending affix. (5 points)

1. raise   +   ing   = _____

2. orange   +   s   = _____

3. crab   +   y   = _____

4. forgive   +   ing   = _____

5. rain   +   y   = _____

G. Read this paragraph.

      Does your state have a sales tax? This tax is the extra money you pay on the things you buy. A sales tax helps your state to stay inside its budget.

In the paragraph above, underline the words that contain the long sound of the letter **a** (ā). (6 points)

H. Listen, then circle the word that the teacher says. (4 points)

1. rise   raise   rose   ruse

2. bran   barn   brine   brain

3. hill   he'll   who'll   hole

4. messed   mast   most   must

I. Circle the *sight word* in each row. (2 points)

1. pay   trays   displays   says

2. strain   claim   straight   wail

Name: _____

A. Divide each word into syllables. Mark the vowel in the *first* syllable as long (ˉ), short (˘), or schwa (ə). (12 points—2 points each)

	First Syllable	Second Syllable		First Syllable	Second Syllable
1. adult	_____	_____	**4.** amend	_____	_____
2. bottom	_____	_____	**5.** tuna	_____	_____
3. sofa	_____	_____	**6.** sudden	_____	_____

B. Join each word and its ending affix. (5 points)

1. amuse + ing = _____

2. settle + ment = _____

3. red + est = _____

4. amuse + ment = _____

5. settle + er = _____

C. Fill in each blank. (4 points)

1. The root word of *taped* is _____.

2. The root word of *furry* is _____.

3. The root word of *gambler* is _____.

4. The root word of *widest* is _____.

Student Book 3
Part 2 *cont.*
(50 points)

D. Match each word in Column A with its definition in Column B. Write the letter of your answer on the line next to the number. (10 points)

Column A	*Column B*
____ **1.** among	**a.** wide awake; watchful
____ **2.** dozen	**b.** to chase; to go after
____ **3.** nothing	**c.** maybe
____ **4.** furnish	**d.** in the middle of
____ **5.** alert	**e.** up-to-date; at the present time
6. pursue	**f.** to rule
____ **7.** govern	**g.** to supply; to provide; to equip
____ **8.** urban	**h.** twelve
____ **9.** perhaps	**i.** related to a city; having to do with a city
____ **10.** current	**j.** not anything

E. Read this paragraph.

A person trained in first aid can help victims of snake bites, burns, or choking. Most of the time, a victim must not be moved until medical help can be obtained. Victims who have been hurt also must be kept warm.

In the paragraph above, circle the words that contain the sound of /ŭr/. (4 points)

Student Book 3
Part 2 *cont.*
(50 points)

F. Choose the correct word and write it in the blank. (4 points)

1. The planet Mars is _____ (smaller, smallest) than Venus.

2. Portland is the _____ (larger, largest) city in Maine.

3. Today is the _____ (hotter, hottest) day of the summer.

4. Rachel can work _____ (quicker, quickest) than the other nurses.

G. Listen, then circle the word that the teacher says. (5 points)

1. cave   crave   carve   curve

2. biker   bicker   backer   baker

3. ton   tone   tune   tan

4. dune   done   din   dine

5. banned   bend   bond   boned

H. Circle the two words that contain a scribal **o.** (2 points)

some   hotel   broke   robot   job   front

I. Read the sentence below. Add apostrophes and punctuation marks. (4 points)

Doesnt Mr Miller go to work at seven oclock

A. Read this paragraph.

I was flying home. The plane dipped as it began to come in for a landing. From high above, I could see the bright lights of the city blinking in the night. I smiled to myself. The lights seemed to be saying, "Welcome home!"

In the paragraph above, circle the words that contain the long *i* sound. (11 points)

B. Fill in each blank with the correct word. (4 points)

1. Do you _____ (think, thought) that your boss will give me a job?

2. She _____ (buy, bought) four tickets for the concert on Friday night.

3. The night watchman _____ (bring, brought) his dog to guard the front gate.

4. Two boxers will _____ (fight, fought) at the Athletic Club next week.

C. Divide these words into syllables with a slash (/). (6 points)

1. needle _____

2. nighttime _____

3. freedom _____

4. coastline _____

5. lightning _____

6. asleep _____

D. Write the contraction for each combination. (4 points)

1. I would _____

2. should have _____

3. they would _____

4. could not _____

E. Join each word and its ending affix. (7 points)

1. study   +   ed   =   _____

2. happy   +   ly   =   _____

3. pity   +   ful   =   _____

4. hurry   +   ing   =   _____

5. pretty   +   est   =   _____

6. attorney   +   s   =   _____

7. story   +   s   =   _____

F. Use a word in the parentheses to fill in the blank. (4 points)

1. (hopeful, hopeless) The doctors are _____ that she will fully recover by next month.

2. (painful, painless) The nurse gave me a _____ shot in the arm. It didn't hurt at all!

3. (harmful, harmless) A lot of sun may be _____ to your skin.

4. (restful, restless) At 5:00 P.M., I became _____.

G. Match each word in Column A with its definition in Column B. (6 points)

Column A	Column B
____ **1.** steel	**a.** the upper part of the leg
____ **2.** slept	**b.** a gentle wind
____ **3.** thigh	**c.** past tense of bleed
____ **4.** oath	**d.** a strong metal
____ **5.** breeze	**e.** past tense of sleep
____ **6.** bled	**f.** a sworn statement to tell the truth; a pledge

H. Draw a line from each word in the left column to its definition in the right column. (4 points)

soar	public way for travel; a highway; a freeway
sore	to fly or glide high
road	past tense of ride
rode	painful and tender

I. Listen, then circle the word that the teacher says. (3 points)

1. boat   bought   but   bat   bait

2. ought   oat   oath   ate   at

3. sleep   slip   slap   slop   slope

J. One word below is *not* a sight word. Circle that word. (1 point)

write   many   been   roast   knee   broad

A. Write the plural form (more than one) of each word. (7 points)

1. tour _____

2. couch _____

3. country _____

4. blouse _____

5. mountain _____

6. mouse _____

7. county _____

B. Fill in each blank with a word from the box below. (6 points)

courses courthouse cousin hour our soup

1. Wiley is taking a couple of _____ at the local college.

2. The file clerk was one _____ late getting to work.

3. My attorney will meet the judge at the county _____.

4. She almost always has _____ and salad for lunch.

5. On Thursday, we're taking _____ son to the clinic for his shots.

6. His young _____ got a ticket for running a red light.

C. Read the sentence below. Add capital letters, an apostrophe, and punctuation marks. The entire sentence must be correct for credit. (1 point)

dr roberts couldnt remove the stitches on friday

D. Write the ABBREVIATION for each word below. (7 points)

1. second _____

2. minute _____

3. hour _____

4. ounce _____

5. pound _____

6. mile _____

7. miles per hour _____

E. Match each word in Column A with its definition in Column B. Write the letter of your answer on the line. (6 points)

Column A

____ **1.** detour

____ **2.** young

____ **3.** couple

____ **4.** scour

____ **5.** sour

____ **6.** thousand

Column B

a. not old

b. having a sharp, strong taste, like a lemon

c. to scrub; to rub hard

d. 10 x 100

e. a roundabout route that takes the place of the main route

f. two

F. Divide these words into syllables. Mark the vowels in each syllable long (-), short (˘), or schwa (ə). (6 points)

	First Syllable	Second Syllable			First Syllable	Second Syllable
1. panic	_____	_____	4. extra	_____	_____
2. lotto	_____	_____	5. comet	_____	_____
3. item	_____	_____	6. adapt	_____	_____

G. Read this paragraph.

Do you like ghost stories? If you do, you're not alone. Most of us love creepy tales about monsters, demons, and vampires. Many times, these stories take place in a graveyard on a foggy night or during a thunderstorm on a lonely road. We wait for the moment when something frightful will happen.

Read the paragraph again and circle all the words that contain the sound of long **o** (ō). (8 points)

H. Fill in each blank with the correct word. (4 points)

1. The root word for *happiness* is _____.

2. The root word for *unwashable* is _____.

3. The root word for *rehired* is _____.

4. The root word for *unsnapping* is _____.

I. In each row, circle the *sight word*. (2 points)

1. about   mouth   doubt   cloud   pouch

2. restless   sleepiness   darkness   business   sadness

J. Listen, then circle the word that the teacher says. (3 points)

1. house   hose   whose

2. shut   shot   shout

3. bought   bout   boat